GREEK CONNECTIONS:
ESSAYS ON CULTURE AND DIPLOMACY

*THE STEPHEN J., SR.,
AND BEATRICE BRADEMAS LECTURES
1976–1986*

Mr. Stephen J. Brademas, Sr., 1975

Mrs. Beatrice Brademas, 1985

Greek Connections:
Essays on Culture and Diplomacy

Edited by
JOHN T. A. KOUMOULIDES

Foreword by
JOHN BRADEMAS

University of Notre Dame Press
Notre Dame, Indiana

Copyright © 1987 by
University of Notre Dame Press
Notre Dame, Indiana 46556
All Rights Reserved

Library of Congress Cataloging in Publication Data

Greek connections.

"The Stephen J. Sr. and Beatrice Brademas lectures, 1976-1986"—Half t.p.
1. Greece—Civilization. 2. Greece—History.
I. Koumoulides, John T. A., 1938-   . II. Title: Stephen J. Sr. and Beatrice Brademas lectures.
DF741.G72   1987   949.5   87-11266
ISBN 0-268-01014-5 (pbk.)

Manufactured in the United States of America

To Beatrice Brademas

"Nescio qua natale solum dulcedine captos Ducit,
et immemores non sinit esse sui."

By some strange charm our native land doth
hold us captive,
nor permits that we should e'er forget her.

Ovid *Epistolae ex Ponto* 1.3.135

Contents

Foreword • JOHN BRADEMAS	ix
Preface • JOHN T. A. KOUMOULIDES	xi
Contributors	xv
Polybius between Greece and Rome • FERGUS G. B. MILLAR	1
The Hellenism of Zenobia • GLEN W. BOWERSOCK	19
The Reception of Greek Literature in Armenia • ROBERT W. THOMSON	28
The Byzantine Missions of Saints Cyril and Methodius • DIMITRI OBOLENSKY	44
The Image of Greece in Modern English Literature • ASA BRIGGS	58
Tsarist Russia and Greek Independence • BARBARA JELAVICH	75
Cyprus: A Failure in Western Diplomacy • NANCY CRAWSHAW	102
Education—The International Dimension • JOHN BRADEMAS	117

Foreword

I take great personal pleasure in introducing this collection of essays, first delivered as the Stephen J., Sr., and Beatrice Brademas Lectures at Ball State University.

The publication of this volume, marking the first decade of the Brademas lecture series, represents a proud moment for my family. It was early in this century that, at the age of twenty-one, my late father, Stephen J. Brademas, left Calamata, Greece, eventually to settle in South Bend, Indiana. In Mishawaka, Indiana, my father met my mother, Beatrice Cenci Goble; they married and raised four children — my brothers Tom and Jim, my sister Eleanor Keb, and me.

That a lecture series should have been established in my parents' names, in the state in which they made their home, and, moreover, at a university with which my family has had so many links, would have greatly pleased my father. My mother continues to be deeply gratified by this tribute to her beloved husband and herself. The appearance of this book also reinforces my family's relationship with two fine universities in my native state of Indiana.

My late grandfather, William Chester Goble, my mother's father, taught summer courses between 1923 and 1926 at Ball State University (then Ball Teachers College); and my mother was at three different times a student there. In addition, I was privileged in 1973 to be awarded an honorary degree by Ball State.

That these lectures should be published by the University of Notre Dame Press is also fitting. For the Brademas children grew up, and our family lived our lives, in the shadow of the

Golden Dome. My own long-time mentor, valued friend, and now academic colleague is the Reverend Theodore M. Hesburgh, C.S.C., for thirty-five years the president of Notre Dame.

That this series was the result of the inspiration and tenacity of purpose of a young scholar who had become not only a close friend but almost part of our family would have especially pleased my father. On behalf of the entire Brademas family, I express profound gratitude to Professor John T. A. Koumoulides, for without his energy and effort these lectures and this book would not have been possible. Not only is Dr. Koumoulides himself a prolific researcher and writer in the field of Greek history and culture but, through the lectures represented in this volume, he has brought to the Ball State campus some of the world's most eminent scholars of Greece.

As I observe in the final essay, because I am a child of both Greece and the United States, I have been particularly interested in the development of Greek studies and programs, like the Brademas lectures, in this country. I am encouraged that Americans now recognize not only the greatness of classical Greece, first love of philhellenes everywhere, but also the richness of the Byzantine era and the many exciting contributions of contemporary Greece. Courses and lectures covering the three periods—classical, Byzantine, and modern Greece—are now offered at colleges and universities all over the United States.

Greek Connections: Essays on Culture and Diplomacy embraces a wide span of Greek history and civilization, and the authors reflect the most respected thought in their fields. I hope the book will not only attract the attention of philhellenes but will move others to discover for themselves the glory that continues to be Greece.

JOHN BRADEMAS
PRESIDENT, NEW YORK UNIVERSITY

Preface

"Graecia capta ferum victorem cepit et artis intulit agresti Latio." Greece subdued, captivated her uncivilised conqueror, and imported her arts into unpolished Latium.
Horace *Epistles* 2.1.156

The Stephen J., Sr., and Beatrice Brademas Scholarship and Lecture Fund had its genesis in 1976. The Fund was established at Ball State University in Muncie, Indiana, in honor of the late Stephen Brademas and his wife, Beatrice, who lives in Mishawaka, Indiana.

The purpose of the Fund is twofold: first, through education and cultural exchanges, to promote understanding and appreciation of the history and culture of Greece, as well as to contribute to the strengthening of the traditional bonds of friendship between the peoples of the United States of America and Greece; second, through a series of lectures, to bring to Ball State University, the city of Muncie, and the state of Indiana outstanding individuals to enrich our knowledge and deepen our understanding of the civilization and culture of Greece from ancient times to the present.

In the decade 1976–1986, distinguished students of Greece from Europe and the United States came to Ball State University and lectured on different aspects of Greek history and civilization. Under the auspices of the Brademas Fund, the following scholars delivered lectures: the Hon. Sir Steven Runciman, CH.; Sir Ronald Syme, OM.; the Rt. Hon. Lord Caradon; Sir David Hunt; Sir Edward Peck; Dr. Joseph Gill, S.J.; the Hon. C. M. Woodhouse; and Professors John E. Rexine, John Anton, Donald Nicol, and Giles Constable. Their papers have been published elsewhere.* Professors Angeliki Laiou, James H. Billington, and Constantine Trypanis also appeared at Ball State University under the Brademas Lecture program.

The authors who contributed to *Greek Connections* add a scholarly perspective to our knowledge of Greece and powerfully illustrate the impact of Greece beyond its geographic frontiers. Greek civilization and Greek institutions, classical and Byzantine—ideological, political, architectural, artistic, literary—have long been the admiration and inspiration of other cultures and societies across the continents. These essays persuasively demonstrate our extraordinary debt to the world of Hellas and to the Hellenes.

The publication of *Greek Connections* is also both a tribute to the late Stephen J. Brademas, Sr., and a celebration of a decade of scholarship. *Greek Connections* is dedicated to Beatrice Brademas in gratitude for her generous support of the lecture series since its beginning.

I record as well my great appreciation to the children of Stephen and Beatrice Brademas—Dr. John Brademas, Mr. T. Brooks Brademas, Dr. D. James Brademas, and Mrs. Eleanor Keb—for their moral and financial support of the lectures. I am also most grateful for the support the lectures have received from loyal friends of the Brademas family such as Senator Paul S. Sarbanes, Representative Lee H. Hamilton, Mr. George P. Livanos, Professor Giles Constable, and others in the United States; the Hon. Sir Steven Runciman, CH., Lord Caradon, Sir Ronald Syme, OM., Sir David and Lady Hunt in the United Kingdom, Professor and Mrs. Constantine Tsatsos, and Mr. Angelos Canellopoulos of Greece, as well as others. The distinguished participants' gracious and enthusiastic

---

*See J. Koumoulides, ed., *Cyprus in Transition, 1960–1985* (1986); idem, *Greece and Cyprus in History* (1985); D. Hoover and J. Koumoulides, eds., *Conspectus of History: Family History* (1980); idem, *Conspectus of History: Focus on Interpretation of History* (1978); idem, *Conspectus of History: Cities in History* (1977); Giles Constable, *Attitudes Toward Self-Inflicted Suffering in the Middle Ages* (1982); and Donald Nicol, *Greece and Byzantium* (1983).

Preface

acceptance of our invitation is deeply appreciated by the editor and the Brademas family.

Thanks are also due the president, faculty, and students of Ball State University as well as to the people of Muncie, and in particular Dr. and Mrs. Philip Ball, and Professor and Mrs. Richard Burkhardt for their warm *philoxenia* extended to members of the Brademas family and the visitors.

Finally, I am most grateful to James R. Langford, Director of the University of Notre Dame Press, for his effective support of the publication of this book and to Carole Roos for her editorial assistance.

Ἀνδρί τοι χρεών μνήμην προσεῖναι, τερπνόν εἴ τί που πάθοι. If a man has received a kindness from another, he ought ever to keep it in grateful remembrance. —Sophocles.

J.T.A.K.

Contributors

JOHN BRADEMAS is President of New York University. For twenty-two years (1959–1981) he served as United States Representative in Congress from Indiana's Third District, the last four as House Majority Whip, third-ranking member of the Majority Leadership. He is the author of *Anarcosindicalismo y revolución en España, 1930–1937* (1974), *Washington, D.C. to Washington Square* (1986), *The Politics of Education: Conflicts and Consensus on Capitol Hill* (1987), and of numerous essays, reviews, and articles. Dr. Brademas is a Corresponding Member of the Academy of Athens.

THE RT. HON. LORD BRIGGS is Provost of Worcester College, University of Oxford. He is the author of *A Social History of England* (1983).

GLEN W. BOWERSOCK is Professor of Ancient History at the Institute for Advanced Study, Princeton. He is the author of *Julian the Apostate* (1978).

NANCY CRAWSHAW is the author of *The Cyprus Revolt: An Account of the Struggle for Union with Greece* (1978).

BARBARA JELAVICH is Professor of History at Indiana University. Her two-volume *History of the Balkans* was published in 1983.

JOHN KOUMOULIDES is Professor of History at Ball State University. His *Churches of Aghia in Larissa,* co-authored with Lazaros Deriziotis and published in Athens, received the Academy of Athens Award in 1985. He is the editor of *Cyprus in Transition, 1960–1985* (1986).

FERGUS MILLAR is the Camden Professor of Ancient History at the University of Oxford, and Fellow of Brasenose College, Oxford. With Erich Segal he edited *Caesar Augustus: Seven Aspects* (1984). He is Fellow of the British Academy.

SIR DIMITRI OBOLENSKY is Fellow of Christ Church, Oxford. His *The Byzantine Commonwealth: Eastern Europe 500–1453* appeared in 1971. He is Fellow of the British Academy and a Corresponding Member of the Academy of Athens.

ROBERT W. THOMSON is Director of Dumbarton Oaks, Washington, D.C. His *Moses Khorenatsi: History of the Armenians* was published in 1978.

Polybius between Greece and Rome
Fergus G. B. Millar

I would like to begin with some much-quoted words of Polybius himself (1.1.5). "For who is so worthless or so idle as not to wish to find out by what steps and overcome by what sort of political structure almost all parts of the inhabited world have, in the space of hardly fifty-three years, fallen under the domination of the Romans, a thing which is not found ever to have happened before?"

The fifty-three years which Polybius refers to were those which began in 220 B.C., the moment when, in his view, events in all parts of the Hellenized world, previously separate, began to be interconnected; they ended in 168 B.C., when, at the battle of Pydna, Rome destroyed the first of the great Hellenistic monarchies, that of the Antigonids, which had ruled Macedonia for a little over a century. By "domination" (*arche*) Polybius did not mean what we often mean when we think of the formation of the Roman Empire: the creation of territorial provinces and the imposition of tribute. He meant military victory, the right to decide whether or in what form a city or a kingdom might keep its independence, and the ability to command obedience by the threat of force.[1]

That same year, 168 B.C., saw the most spectacular of all examples of the exercise of Roman domination in this sense. Antiochus IV, the ruler of the Seleucid Kingdom, based on Syria and Babylonia, had invaded Egypt, had defeated the Ptolemies, had claimed the kingship of Egypt for himself,[2] and was outside Alexandria with his army. But at that moment there appeared a Roman ambassador, Popilius Laenas, who handed the king the text of a decree of the Senate, telling him to end his war with Egypt. When the king said that he would consult with his advisers, Laenas made the famous gesture of drawing a circle in the sand round where the king was standing, and telling him to give his answer before stepping out of it. The king submitted. The earliest narrative of this famous scene comes from Polybius himself (29.27). But the humiliation of the king made an immediate impact in the Eastern Mediterranean, as we know from a pseudo-prophecy in the book of Daniel, written only a couple of years later (11:30): "For the ships of Kittim will come, and he shall be grieved and return."

While the two Ptolemies were still in danger from Antiochus IV's advance, the major league of Greek cities in the Peloponnese, the Achaean League, had debated whether to send military assistance to them. Ambassadors from the two Ptolemies, brothers who were formerly at odds but now reconciled, had arrived asking for the dispatch of 1,000 footsoldiers and 200 cavalry. The infantry were to be commanded by Lycortas, the father of Polybius, and the cavalry by Polybius himself, now probably in his thirties.[3] The proposal, however, ran into difficulties; the pro-Roman party argued that all their efforts should be directed to helping the Romans in their current war against Perseus, the King of Macedon, in which a decisive battle was now (rightly) expected. Polybius replied that in the previous year (169 B.C.), when he had been sent as ambassador to the Roman commander, he had been told that the Romans needed no military assistance; in any case the Achaean League could raise 30,000 or even 40,000 men if need be, so 1,000 going off to Alexandria would make no difference (29.23–25).

In fact the force was not sent to Alexandria. In the same year, 168 B.C., the Romans defeated the Macedonians at Pydna, and the kingdom was dissolved. In the following year large numbers of political figures in Greece, regarded as anti-Roman, were taken off to exile in Rome and Italy: among these were 1,000 from Achaea, including Polybius himself. They were to remain there for seventeen years until their eventual release in 150 B.C.

It was in Rome that Polybius conceived his enormously ambitious plan for a universal history which would, first, show how events in all the different parts of the civilized (i.e. Hellenized) world came together in a set of causal interconnections, from 220 B.C. onwards. It would therefore cover an unprecedented geographical range, from Antiochus III's campaigns in northern India in the last decade of the third century to the Roman wars in Spain. The work was also on an enormous scale in itself. Had it survived complete, it would have run to over 4,000 printed pages of a Teubner text, or twenty Loeb volumes. As it is, what remains occupies six Loeb volumes. This always has to be remembered when we speak of what Polybius thought—or what he seems to have omitted.

One reason the work was so long was that Polybius changed his mind about where it should end. The original stopping point was to be the destruction of the Macedonian kingdom in 168 B.C. But at the beginning of Book 3 he describes why he changed his mind:

> Now, if from their success or failure alone we could form an adequate judgment of how far states or individuals are worthy of praise or blame, I could here lay down my pen. . . . For the period of fifty-three years finished here and the growth and advance of Roman power was now complete. . . . But since judgments regarding either the conquerors or the conquered based purely on performance are by no means final . . . I must append to the history of the above period an account of the subsequent policy of the conquerors and their method of universal rule, as well as of the various opinions and appreciations of these rulers entertained by the subjects (3.4).

He therefore, in this second introduction, sketches the events which were to occupy the last ten books (30–39), covering the years from 167 to 146 B.C. The culminating point was to be the war of 147–146 B.C., in which the Achaean League rose in revolt against Rome and was destroyed. It is crucial to his whole historical perspective that he chose the tragic end of his own league as his conclusion; this, along with the Roman defeat of a renewed revolt in Macedon, was "the general disaster of all Hellas" (3.5.6).

Polybius' second intention, in his original plan, had been not merely to describe how all these complex events interlocked, but to explain why the Romans had been successful. The explanation, as the quotation with which this essay begins indicated, was to be in terms of the Roman constitution or political structure, the *politeia:* "Who would not wish to find out . . . what sort of *politeia* had enabled the Romans to achieve domination of the whole civilised world?" The reference is of course to the famous analysis of the working of the Roman constitution and political system in Book 6, which he placed just after the Romans' most crushing defeat, by Hannibal at Cannae in 216 B.C. This in other words was the moment when, if there were weaknesses in the system, they would show up. In fact the Roman system, with its elaborate checks and balances, showed remarkable resilience, and Hannibal was ultimately defeated.

As to the question of whether Polybius' analysis of Rome was appropriate or wholly misguided, my view is that it was not in the least inappropriate to discuss Rome in terms of Greek political theory, or to compare it to well-known Greek models.[4] But my main point is that to understand Polybius we have to accept that his whole perspective is that of the self-governing Greek city, or league, of the classical and Hellenistic periods. The second point is that Polybius' intention, in analyzing the reasons for the success of Rome, was neutral: to give reasons for success and resilience is not in itself to recommend a system, still less to praise the results of its success.

That brings me to a third preliminary point. In going on to cover the troubled period from 167 to 146 B.C., Polybius evidently did intend to introduce an element of moral judgment into his *History.* How in fact had the victors used their power? There is no simple or unambiguous way of stating Polybius' conclusion. In a paper with the same title as this one, F. W. Walbank, the greatest modern expert on Polybius, concluded that on the whole his view was favorable.[5] I think otherwise; that Polybius, though he expresses himself obliquely took an increasingly distant and hostile view of Roman domination.

At the very least, one point is surely remarkable by its absence. In the whole surviving text there is not a single word to the effect that Roman domination was a good thing or brought benefits to those who came under it. For a man who believed that the Achaean revolution of 147–146 B.C. was a tragic error, who had spent seventeen years in Rome, and who had friends in the highest Roman circles, this silence surely speaks volumes.

There is more to it than that, however. In the second to last of the surviving books (38) he comes to the Achaean war of 147–146 B.C., which destroyed his own Achaean League, which he had called in Book 2 the political system best fitted of all for equality and freedom of speech — in fact, true democracy (2.38.6). To introduce it he puts it deliberately in a long historical perspective: going back to Xerxes' invasion of Greece in 480 B.C., he reviews all the major calamities and conflicts in Greek history, and concludes that this was the greatest disaster of all; partly because it was the Achaeans' own fault, partly because in other cases no moral blame had been incurred, and partly because recovery from disaster had often come swiftly. This time, by implication, no recovery was in sight (38.2–3).

To Polybius the role of the historian was not just to record, though a history which recorded events on a universal scale gained great significance from that alone. The historian's role was to judge, to put events in a wider context, and to provide lessons for the future. For that of course the historian must himself have political and military experience; Polybius had a leading role in a major Greek league. Second, he must be able to see the events he is recording in perspective and, by setting them in context, to bring out their meaning and significance. In the quotation from the first two pages of Polybius with which I began, he suggests that no one could be so indolent as not to want to understand how Rome had achieved universal domination. The significance of that domination would become clear, however, by comparison with the empires of the past:

> The Persians for a certain period possessed a great rule and dominion, but so often as they ventured to overstep the boundaries of Asia they

imperilled not only the security of their empire but their own existence. The Lacedaimonians, after having for many years disputed the hegemony of Greece, at length attained it but to hold it uncontested for some twelve years. The Macedonian rule in Europe extended but from the Adriatic region to the Danube. . . . Subsequently, by overthrowing the Persian empire they became supreme in Asia also. But . . . they never even made a single attempt to dispute possession of Sicily, Sardinia, or Libya, and the most warlike nations of Western Europe were, to speak the simple truth, unknown to them (1.2).

In this last sentence he is emphasizing a distinctive feature of Roman domination. It is not of course wrong to see Polybius as a historian of Rome and its empire. Indeed when Penguin Books recently brought out a one-volume selection of Polybius, they called it *The Rise of the Roman Empire,* and made the selection in such a way as to concentrate almost entirely on Roman history. However, to do that, though it has its uses, is to lose sight of Polybius' vastly wider geographical perspective of events from India to Asia Minor, to Syria, Egypt, Crete, and Macedonia. But above all it is to neglect the real historical perspective which Polybius brings to the events of his age. That is the perspective, first, of the Greek historical tradition of the classical and Hellenistic periods. It is worth reminding ourselves that these words, "classical" and "Hellenistic," are our terms, not his. They can, moreover, be seriously misleading. Books are still occasionally published which announce that the death of Alexander the Great in 323 B.C. marked the end of Greek freedom, the death of the Greek city-state, and the beginning of a new age.[6] As regards the Hellenization of the East, there was something in this, even though that Hellenization neither began with Alexander nor depended entirely on his conquests.[7] But that was not in any case an aspect of history in which Polybius took much interest. As regards mainland Greece, Hellas proper, it is nonsense.

For Polybius, as is absolutely clear, Greek history from the fifth century to his own time was a continuum, in which there had been many disasters but no violent break. This perspective, as we shall see, stretched back to include some mythical founders and lawgivers, like Lycurgus in Sparta, and it of course reached to the poems of Homer. But the later archaic period, on the evidence of the surviving text, did not play a large part in Polybius' consciousness; nor did the monarchies of the Near East, except by way of general allusions to the Persian Empire. His real historical starting point, or boundary, was Xerxes' invasion of 480 B.C. From that point Polybius' use of earlier history embodies an awareness of a continuous and still relevant story, all of which was of importance for the present. For instance, when he has narrated the Roman defeat of the Gauls in the Po Valley in the 220s B.C., he turns immediately to Greek examples of the successful repulse of barbarians. One of them, once again, is Xerxes' invasion; the other is the defeat of those Gauls who invaded Greece and reached Delphi in 279 B.C., a defeat celebrated throughout the Hellenistic world[8] (he omits to say that the victory was gained by the Aetolians, of whom he did not approve). His motives for making these allusions are, as usual, stated with great clarity:

> For indeed I consider that the writers who chronicled and handed down to us the story of the Persian invasion of Greece and the attack of the Gauls on Delphi have made no small contributions to the struggle of the Hellenes for their common liberty. For there is no one whom hosts of men or abundance of arms or vast resources could frighten into abandoning his last hope, that is to fight to the end for his native land, if he . . . bore in mind how many myriads of men, what determined courage and what armaments were brought to nought by the resolve and power of those who faced the danger with intelligence and coolness (2.35.7–8).

What determines Polybius' perspective is both a national tradition of Greek patriotism and, as this passage illustrates, a historiographical tradition.

As it happens, the surviving text of Polybius nowhere names Herodotus, on whom of course the tradition of the defeat of Xerxes depended. The writers of the later fifth, fourth, and third centuries, Thucydides, Xenophon, Ephorus, Theopompus, Callisthenes, and Timaeus, to name only the major figures, represented for him a continuous tradition of Greek history-writing, to which he constantly makes explicit reference. Indeed his choice of the date 264 B.C., with which he opens his preliminary narrative of Roman history, before he comes to the great conjunction of events in 220–216 B.C., was determined partly by the fact that it was then that Roman forces first crossed into Sicily; and partly by the fact that it was in that year that Timaeus' *History* had stopped (1.51.1; 39.8.4). Nor was there any doubt what the proper and central subject of a Greek history should be. This is made quite clear in what he says of Theopompus' *History,* which covered the period from 411 B.C. to the reign of Philip of Macedon:

> No one could approve of the general scheme of this writer. Having set himself the task of writing the history of Greece from the point at which Thucydides leaves off, just when he was approaching the battle of Leuctra and the most brilliant period of Greek history, he abandoned Greece and her efforts, and changing his plan decided to write the history of Philip. Surely it would have been much more dignified and fairer to include Philip's achievements in the history of Greece than to include the history of Greece in that of Philip (8.11.3–4).

As we shall see at the end, the tension between monarchic power, with its varied threats and possible benefits, and the freedom of the Greek cities was one of the fundamental issues which shaped Polybius' historical consciousness. There is a very real sense in which the period of Greek history within which Polybius most fully "belongs" is that which begins in the very late fifth century, and is marked by the rise and influence of monarchs, whether tyrants, like Dionysius I the tyrant of Syracuse (406–367 B.C.), or kings, like Philip of Macedon and his successors.[9] If we allow ourselves to gain a sense of Polybius' historical consciousness, we might begin to feel more sympathy for the suggestion made by Hermann Bengtson that we should use the term "Hellenistic" not just of the period after Alexander, but from the first half of the fourth century onwards.[10] What Polybius does not do, however, is to treat the monarchies which played such an important part in his world as being themselves objects worthy of the serious application of political theory. In that he is quite explicitly the heir of the fourth-century Greek political theory of Plato and Aristotle, to both of whom he refers repeatedly, and whose analyses were devoted to the nuclear city-state.[11] When he comes to his famous discussion of the Roman constitution in Book 6, the frame of reference or comparison which he applies is first of all Sparta and the constitution given by Lycurgus (6.10); later he returns to Sparta, once again, along with the cities of Crete, Mantinea, and Carthage. Two other candidates for consideration, Athens and Thebes, are set aside because their respective periods of dominance, in the fifth and fourth centuries respectively, were too brief, their political structures too unstable or fragile to be worth serious comparison with that of Rome (6.43–44). In the end, Polybius makes clear, what demonstrated that the Spartan constitution was also inferior to the Roman one was the fact that it did not stand up to the strains imposed on it by controlling a foreign empire. The Spartans had succeeded in dominating their neighbors in the Peloponnese, the Messenians. But when it came, in the early fourth century, to a general domination of Greece, they found themselves compelled to be dependent on the very Persians whom they had just defeated. For they needed to ask them for the funds which their own laws, laid down by Lycurgus, prevented them from generating at home. So they made the inglorious Peace of Antalcidas (the "King's Peace") of 387 B.C., in which they betrayed the freedom of the Greeks to Persia in return for financial support. By comparison, the Romans, having sought at first only the domination of Italy, could command the resources to control an overseas empire as well (6.49–50).[11]

In examining the ability of a city-state to support an empire, Polybius extends the range of political thought beyond that inherited from Plato and Aristotle. So he does also in his marvellous account in Book 2 (37–44) of the history of his own Achaean League from its legendary origins, to its overshadowing by Sparta and then Macedon in the fourth century, and its re-emergence, recovery of freedom, and rapid extension in the third. Plato and Aristotle had not given any attention to analyzing the nature of federal states. Polybius did. By his own time, he says, the Achaean League had almost become a single city-state: "They have the same laws, weights, measures and coinage, as well as the same magistrates, councillors and juries, and the whole Peloponnese only falls short of being a single city in the fact of its inhabitants not being enclosed by one wall" (2.37.10–11).

As has often been noted, Polybius discusses Rome also in terms of a nuclear city-state, and did not devote any attention, so far as we know from the surviving text, to what moderns sometimes call the "Italian confederation." But in that he was in fact right, for the structure of Roman Italy was that of a set of alliances between Rome and individual city-states and peoples, and was no sort of league of confederation like the Achaean League.[12] Where he might have extended the range of political analysis beyond that inherited from Plato and Aristotle was in relation to monarchy. For while the resilience of Rome in the face of three major defeats by Hannibal in the years 218–216 B.C. rightly impressed him, he might well have been struck, by comparison, by the fragility of the great Hellenistic kingdoms, which would admit defeat in a war after the loss of a single battle, as Macedon did in 197 B.C. and 168 B.C., or two battles, as with those of 190 B.C. and 189 B.C., by which the Romans drove Antiochus III first out of Greece and then out of Asia Minor.

Perhaps we should not blame Polybius for this oversight, however, but even the most brilliant of modern accounts, say by Elias Bickermann or Claire Préaux,[13] have hardly succeeded in explaining what a Hellenistic monarchy was really like as a system, or how it held together at all. Confronted with monarchies, Polybius turns either to explanations in terms of personal character or to observations on the instability of human fortune. In both approaches, once again, the framework is supplied by the earlier history of Greece. For instance, when he wants to set in context the fact that Philip V of Macedon in 218 B.C. allowed his army to destroy colonnades and statues in the Aetolian city of Thermon, he reflects on the models which the king should have followed: Philip II's clemency to the Athenians after the battle of Chaeronea in 338 B.C.; Alexander's care not to destroy the temples of Thebes in Boeotia in 335 B.C., or his preservation of temples in the Persian empire (5.10). But Philip V, he says, was either too young or had the wrong advisers, and lost the chance of gaining the good reputation which mercy would have won him (5.11–12). Later Polybius represents Philip V, now much older and perhaps wiser, telling his sons to read tragedies, myths, and histories, and to think of the disastrous effects of strife between brothers; or, alternatively, to think of the kings of Sparta, whose success had been gained by mutual concord and obedience to the laws and the ephors. There was also the contemporary example of the two brothers, Eumenes II and Attalus II of Pergamon, whose concord had raised their kingdoms to greatness from small beginnings (23.11).

When he comes to the great event with which I began, the Roman defeat of Perseus, King of Macedon, at Pydna in 168 B.C., and to the end of the Macedonian monarchy, Polybius turns back again to the fourth century, and quotes a marvellous passage from Demetrius of Phalerum, the philosopher who was the effective ruler of Athens for a decade in the very early Hellenistic period, from 317 to 307 B.C. Demetrius in his work *On Fortune* had reflected on the sudden end of the Persian empire:

> Do you think, that fifty years ago either the Persians and the Persian King or the Macedonians and the King of Macedon, if some god had foretold the future to them, would ever have believed that at the time when we live the very name of the Persians would have perished utterly—the Persians who were masters of almost the whole world—and that the Macedonians, whose name was formerly almost unknown, would now be lords of it all? But nevertheless Fortune . . . now also . . . makes it clear to all men, by endowing the Macedonians with the whole wealth of Persia, that she has but lent them these blessings until she decides to deal differently with them.

A century and a half later, as Polybius reflects, this inspired prophecy had come true, and Fortune had withdrawn from Macedon the blessings which she had briefly given (29.21).

Such reflections were of course not unique to Polybius. By his time, they had entered Roman culture as well. So, as he himself records, when the Roman general Scipio Aemilianus witnessed the destruction of Carthage in 146 B.C., he recalled the fate of the Empires of Assyria, Media, Persia, and Macedon itself, and quoted two lines from the sixth book of Homer's *Iliad* (448–49):

> A day will come when sacred Troy shall perish,
> And Priam and his people shall be slain.

For Polybius the uses of history did not always need to be on so high a philosophical level as that. Writing for a Greek audience, to record and explain the rise of Rome to universal domination, he could on occasion use cross-references to Greek history purely for dating purposes, that is to anchor events in earlier history in a context which was, or was supposed to be, familiar to his educated readers. It is worth stressing how detailed a familiarity with Greek history he seems to presume. "Who had not read," he says at one point, "that when the Athenians, in conjunction with the Thebans, entered on a war against the Lacedaimonians, sending out a force of ten thousand men and manning a hundred triremes, they decided to meet the expenses by a property-tax, and made a valuation for this purpose of the whole of Attica including the houses and other property?" (2.62.6–7). Whether his audience really did have an immediate recall of this episode or not, it belonged, once again, in the fourth century, to be precise in 378 B.C., at the moment of the foundation of the Second Athenian Confederacy.

When he applies Greek history to Roman history for dating purposes, he normally selects points of reference which were more familiar. So, for instance, the year of the earliest treaty between Rome and Carthage is identified not only as the first year of the annual pair of consuls at Rome, and the year after the expulsion of the Roman kings; it was also "twenty-eight years before the crossing of Xerxes into Greece" (3.22.1–2) — that is, in our terms, 508 B.C. Or again, when the Gauls captured all of Rome except the Capitol, it was the nineteenth year after the battle of Aegospotamoi (which ended the Peloponnesian War, in 405 B.C.), the sixteenth year before the battle of Leuktra (in 371 B.C.), the same year as the Peace of Antalcidas with Persia, and also the same year as that in which Dionysius I, the tyrant of Syracuse, was besieging Rhegium, 387 B.C. (1.6.2). These multiple references can only have been helpful to an audience to whom the details of fourth-century history were familiar. Thanks to the Sicilian historian Timaeus, Polybius' Greek history in the fourth and third centuries also embraced the history of Sicily. One of the many revelations of his history, if we think of it as a Greek history, is that it gives us something rather rare, a perspective which is decidedly non-Athenian, and is instead, first, Peloponnesian and, second, Sicilian.

In the third century too, he can use the same anchoring device, relating the Roman victory at Lake Vadimon in 283 B.C. both to Pyrrhus' crossing into southern Italy in 280 B.C. and to the defeat of the Gauls at Delphi in 279 B.C. (2.20.6).

More significant, however, was the use of examples from Greek history as points of reference for historical and political judgments. Once again, such examples can only be useful if they are familiar and are charged with some meaning for their readers. For example, it might be right, Polybius suggests, to see Hannibal in the light of persons, or whole peoples, whom circumstances had caused to act variably, or contrary to their real character. For instance, Agathocles, tyrant of Syracuse in 316–289 B.C., had been by turns cruel and benevolent; Cleomenes, King of Sparta in the third century (235–222 B.C.), exhibited similar contradictions; the Athenian people behaved differently under the leadership of Aristides and Pericles than they did under Cleon and Chares; so also did the Spartans, under Kings Cleombrotus and Agesilaus, in the early fourth century (9. 23). Again, the examples extend from the fifth century into the Hellenistic period. Examples derived from Herodotus play no part in Polybius' mental framework, at least in the surviving text, which is less than one-third of the original.

What Polybius does use from archaic or legendary Greek history does not derive from Herodotus, but rather from separate traditions about early Sparta and its lawgiver, Lycurgus.

It is these which he applies to Rome and its constitution in Book 6, and these which he also uses in interpreting the role of the great Roman general, Scipio Africanus, commander in Spain against the Carthaginians from 210 B.C. onwards:

> To me it seems that the character and principles of Scipio much resembled those of Lycurgus, the Lacedaimonian legislator. For neither must we suppose that Lycurgus drew up the constitution of Sparta under the influence of superstition and solely prompted by the Pythia, nor that Scipio won such an empire for his country by following the suggestions of dreams and omens. But . . . Lycurgus made his own scheme more acceptable and more easily believed by invoking the oracles of the Pythia in support of projects due to himself, while Scipio similarly made the men under his command more sanguine and more ready to face perilous enterprises by instilling into them the belief that his projects were divinely inspired (10.2.8–12).

But the center of Polybius' historical culture was the experience of the Greek city-states from the fifth century onwards, and above all from the fourth century onwards, the period of the rise and intrusion of monarchic power. Thus, when dealing with the complex and catastrophic events of 147 and 146 B.C., which culminated in the more or less simultaneous destruction by the Romans of Carthage and Corinth, he defends his procedure in taking his narrative backwards and forwards between the two theatres of war by reference to existing histories of fourth-century Greece: "When dealing with Thessalian affairs and the exploits of Alexander of Pherae, they [these historians] interrupt the narrative to tell us of the projects of the Lacedaimonians in the Peloponnese or of those of the Athenians and of what happened in Macedonia or Illyria, and after entertaining us so tell us of the expedition of Iphicrates to Egypt and the excesses committed by Clearchus of Pontus" (38.6.2–3). Once again, these events, mainly of the 360s and 350s B.C., are assumed to be familiar to his readers. The same historical background had also been deployed when Polybius first came to the issue of how the Romans acted in the final war against Carthage, and how their actions should be judged.

Polybius conceals his own opinion by the device of setting

out four different opinions of Rome's conduct which were held in Greece. It should be emphasized, however, that none of the four opinions quoted is positively favorable: of the two more favorable, one held that it was a sign of prudence on the part of the Romans to destroy an ancient enemy when the opportunity offered; and the other maintained that the Romans had committed no actual offense in international law. Of the two unfavorable views, one held that the level of deceit used by the Romans amounted to impiety and a breach of treaty obligations. The other was that the Romans had previously taken their warfare only to the point of forcing their opponents to submit to their orders. But now they were deserting their former principles in favor of a lust for domination (*philarchia*) like that of Athens and Sparta and would come to the same bad end (36.9). Here, too, the history of the fifth and fourth centuries is recalled to the reader.

But the most remarkable and detailed of all the occasions where Polybius makes use of the earlier history of Greece belongs at a previous stage in his narrative; very significantly this is at exactly the point where Roman military force first became a major factor in the life of mainland Greece. In 212 or 211 B.C. the Romans, threatened by an alliance between Philip V of Macedon and Hannibal, themselves made an alliance with the Aetolian League, the major power in northwestern Greece.[14] Then in 210 B.C. ambassadors from Acarnania, which was in alliance with Philip, and from Aetolia, now allied to Rome, presented themselves simultaneously at Sparta, each hoping to persuade the Spartans to join his side. To underline the significance of the occasion, Polybius in Book 9 gives each of the two ambassadors a speech which presents a view of the historic role of the Macedonian monarchy in Greece and the light in which the Roman intervention should be viewed. (There is no way of saying how far the speeches in Polybius resemble anything that was actually said on this occasion, shortly before his birth. What matters is simply what we have in the text, two speeches designed to bring out the significance of a major turning point.)[15]

The Aetolian speaks first and, as so often in the text of Polybius, goes back to the mid fourth century to the capture of Olynthus by Philip II and his suppression of Sparta; then Alexander's destruction of Thebes, and Antipater's victory in the Lamian War of 322 B.C. He then comes to the various Successors who ruled in Greece from the late fourth century onwards: "And who is ignorant of the actions of Cassander, Demetrius and Antigonus Gonatas, all so recent that the memory of them is quite vivid? Some of them by introducing garrisons to cities and others by introducing tyrannies left no city with the right to call itself unenslaved." Finally he comes to the acts of violence which Philip V himself had committed in Greece. In the speech as preserved, apparently almost complete, there is no reference to the Romans, except to say that with their aid Philip was likely to be defeated (9.28–31). Whatever the original speaker in 210 B.C. really said, Polybius could have used this point in his narrative to say something positive about the potential Roman role in Greece. He does not. The real issue, as always, lay elsewhere: the preservation of the freedom of the Greek cities in the face of the threats posed by successive kings and dynasties.

Then the Acarnanian ambassador gives a speech which reviews the same historical period, but from the opposite point of view. Philip II, he says, by defeating the Phocians in the Sacred War, i.e., in 346 B.C., had saved the liberty of Greece. In the Peloponnese Philip had come in response to appeals, and had used his power to arbitrate between Sparta and her enemies. His son Alexander had punished the Persians for their offenses against Greece and "in a word he made Asia subject to Greece." As for later crimes in Greece, it was the Aetolians who were most guilty. It was the Macedonian monarchy of the Antigonids, which ruled from 276 B.C. onwards, which had protected Greece against the northern barbarians. Even Antigonus Doson, King of Macedon, in defeating Sparta herself in 222 B.C., had done so in order to liberate her from a tyrant, namely King Cleomenes.

But now, he goes on later, it is no longer a matter of alliances between Greeks: "But now Greece is threatened with a war against men of a foreign race [the Romans] who intend to enslave her, men whom you [the Aetolians] fancy you are calling in against Philip, but whom you are really calling in against yourselves and the whole of Greece." All Greeks should beware, especially the Spartans who had once thrown into a well the ambassador sent by Xerxes to demand submission and had sent Leonidas to defend the liberty of Greece at Thermopylae. The Romans had already committed atrocities in Greece: "A fine alliance this for anyone to determine to join, and especially for you Lacedaimonians, who, when you conquered the barbarians [i.e., the Persians at Plataea in 479 B.C.] decreed that the Thebans were to pay a tithe to the gods for having decided under compulsion, but alone among the Greeks, to remain neutral during the Persian invasion" (9.32–39).

Once again, whatever the real Acarnanian speaker of 210 B.C. actually said, Polybius certainly had the freedom to select what to put in his own narrative, perhaps even the freedom to invent appropriate words. It is surely significant that at the moment of the first substantial Roman involvement in Greece, he makes a speaker represent them as foreigners intent on enslaving Greece, directly comparable to the Persians, those *barbaroi* whose defeat was the central event in Greek history.

What I want to stress, however, is not the implicit reservations in Polybius' attitude to Rome; though nothing could be more false, in my view, than the idea that, in explaining to the Greek world how and why Rome had gained universal domination, he was also recommending, or even defending, Roman rule. What is important is the fact that Polybius' *History* really is the product of his earlier experience as a central figure in the self-governing Achaean League of cities which occupied a large part of the Peloponnese. To Polybius that part of the past which mattered, that past from which lessons could be drawn, was the experience of the Greek city-states since the victory over Xerxes. It was a continuous history, all of which offered lessons and examples that were relevant to the present. Polybius would have been surprised to learn that something called the

Hellenistic Age had begun in 323 B.C., and that he himself was a Hellenistic historian. He would surely have supposed that he was simply a Greek one.

NOTES

The translations in the text are those of the Loeb edition.

1. See P. S. Derow, "Polybius, Rome and the East," *JRS* 69 (1979): 1.

2. For the now decisive evidence that he had, see J. D. Ray, *The Archive of Hor* (1976), 127.

3. For the most recent argument on the dates of Polybius's life, see M. Dubuisson, "Sur la mort de Polybe," *REG* 93 (1980): 72.

4. For this review, see "The Political Character of the Classical Roman Republic (200–151 B.C.)," *JRS* 74 (1984): 1.

5. F. W. Walbank, "Polybius between Greece and Rome," *Polybe* (Entretiens Hardt 20, 1973), 1.

6. See, e.g., N. G. L. Hammond, *A History of Greece to 322 BC*, 2d. ed. (1967), 651.

7. See, e.g., F. Millar, "The Phoenician cities: a case-study of Hellenisation," *Proc. Camb. Philol. Soc.* 209 (1983): 55.

8. For this, see G. Nachtergael, *les Galates en Grèce et les Sôtéria de Delphes* (1977).

9. For this theme, see esp. J. K. Davies, *Democracy and Classical Greece* (1978), ch. 8.

10. H. Bengtson, *Griechische Geschichte*, 5th ed. (1977), 295 ff.

11. For his explicit allusions to Plato and Aristotle see the Teubner ed. by Th. Büttner-Wobst, 5, pp. 238 (Aristotle) and 242 (Plato).

12. See F. Millar, op. cit. (n. 4).

13. E. J. Bickermann, *Institutions des Séleucides* (1939): C. Préaux, *Le monde hellénistique* 1–2 (1978), 181–294.

14. H. H. Schmitt, *Die Staatsverträge des Altertums* 3 (1969), no. 536.

15. See esp. F. W. Walbank, "Polybius and Rome's Eastern Policy," *JRS* 53 (1963): 1.

The Hellenism of Zenobia
Glen W. Bowersock

The culture of classical Greece radiated outward from the homeland relatively early in the first millennium B.C. Greek colonists and traders carried with them the language, gods, and traditions that comprised the Greek heritage we call Hellenism—a word that is formed from the Greeks' own name for themselves, Hellenes. But it was Alexander the Great, the Macedonian conquerer in the later fourth century B.C., who spread across the entire Near East as far as Afghanistan the Greek culture which he had inherited from his neighbors to the south. Alexander's invasion of the Persian empire was the single most powerful cultural shock in the eastern Mediterranean until the diffusion of Christianity from a corner of Palestine several centuries later. And Christianity itself made its triumphant way throughout the eastern Mediterranean in the Greek language that Alexander had brought to the region and not in the Aramaic of Jesus. The medium through which Christianity was promulgated in the first centuries of our era constitutes an eloquent proof of the strength of the Hellenic traditions introduced by Alexander and his troops.

But Hellenism in no sense supplanted the culture of the Near East. It did not eradicate or distort the deeply rooted ways of the Jews and Arabs who made up the principal Semitic populations of the region. The Semitic traditions were of far greater antiquity than those of the Greeks even in Greece itself, and Aramaic in its various dialects was so widespread a language of communication throughout the Near East that the Persians had adopted it as the international language of their far-flung empire. The cultural confrontation of Greeks with Arabs and Jews was momentous not only in its implications for the history of the eastern Mediterranean but for the history of western civilization overall. The Hellenism that ultimately took root in the West through the Christianization of the Roman Empire was Hellenism that had been compounded with the vital elements of the Near East and transformed by them. The Hellenism of the Judeo-Arab world was visibly faithful to its origins in Greece, and yet it became a recognizably distinct cultural tradition that was no more alien to the eastern peoples than the beliefs and the ways of life of their distant forefathers.

It is a mistake all too frequently repeated to view the Hellenism of the centuries after Alexander the Great as some kind of superimposition on a native culture that maintained, until the arrival of Islam under Muhammad, a tension with indigenous traditions. We moderns have an unfortunate Hegelian weakness in tending to view the events of the past in terms of great struggles between opposing polar forces, and so we think of Christianity against paganism, or of Hellenism against Judaism, or of Hellenism against Islam. In modern times we find it hard to think in other terms than the United States against Russia. Yet this naive and simplistic way of interpreting human events is certainly not a helpful approach for understanding the greatest historical transformations in classical antiquity. The ancients themselves were not inclined to think in such terms because, happily for them, Hegel had not yet existed, and Plato and Aristotle — the Greek philosophers whom everyone knew — were far more subtle. The Christians, those supposed enemies of the pagans, were deeply indebted to the writings of both Plato and Aristotle and were not ashamed to admit it. Obviously an excess of zeal in the cause of Hellenism or paganism or Christianity or Judaism could in individual instances produce open hostility. But a Herod the Great with his extravagantly Greek affectations or a Julian the Apostate with his militant and eccentric paganism should not deflect our attention from the broad meshing of these great forces in the genesis of a coherent social and cultural organism.

I propose to illustrate this general point by reference to one of the most remarkable figures in the entire history of the Roman and Byzantine Near East. Zenobia was an Arab queen who ruled over the caravan city of Palmyra, strategically located at an oasis in the Syrian desert. Between A.D. 270 and 272 she brought the power of her city and the domains under its control to such a height that she was able to challenge the emperor of the entire Roman world. For those two years she laid claim to a share in the imperial rule; and, when the emperor Aurelian was finally compelled to lead a major military expedition against Palmyra, the confrontation was not a cultural one. This was not the Greco-Roman world against the oriental world. Far from it: this was the response of the legitimate emperor to a powerful usurper who made her challenge within the structure and traditions of the empire itself. By her bold challenge to the Roman authority Zenobia has won a place in history alongside other great women of antiquity such as Semiramis and Cleopatra. When Zenobia was captured by Aurelian and taken, as it seems, back to Rome for an appearance in the triumphal celebration of Aurelian's victory over the kingdom of Palmyra, the Romans were themselves so conscious of Zenobia's great qualities of mind and culture that they allowed her to take up a residence in the environs of Tivoli outside Rome, where her name was known and respected for centuries thereafter.[1]

Modern historians have had a difficult time with Zenobia because they have had trouble in separating the usurper, whom they considered a barbarian enemy of Rome, from the heir to Near Eastern traditions of Hellenism that had as deep roots in Palmyra as anywhere in the entire area. It seemed all too easy to the Hegelian mind to assume that the conflict between Zenobia and Aurelian was simply the conflict of East and West, of the Orient against Rome, of the desert against the cultivated lands, of Semitic gods against Greco-Roman gods. But such interpretations miss the important lesson of cultural interaction and diffusion.

Palmyra had become a wealthy and influential city through

its exploitation of the caravan trade from the Persian Gulf to the Mediterranean as well as overland across the Euphrates and on to the Mediterranean. The city's resources had allowed it to develop an extensive network of desert patrols that protected the caravans from marauders, and this policing of the remote desert frontier proved, naturally enough, to be an important part of the defense system of the whole eastern Roman Empire. When, in the middle of the third century A.D., a Roman emperor was defeated and actually taken captive by the Persians, it became apparent to the central administration in Rome that the resources of Palmyra would henceforth be essential to protect Rome's own interests. Accordingly, the leaders of the desert city acquired, quite legitimately, recognition from the Roman government as its surrogates in the Syrian desert. Zenobia's husband had a formal title conferred upon him by Rome in recognition of his official role in monitoring the eastern frontier.[2] And so when her husband died, the power and authority devolved upon Zenobia herself.

Observing the weakness of the Roman administration in the late A.D. 260s, Zenobia gave rein to her own ambitions. She was not the first ally and deputy of the Romans to decide that she could do the job of imperial rule better than the emperor. Her decision to rebel fits perfectly well within the context of usurpation in the third century A.D. What she envisaged for the new era can be seen from the kind of court she assembled at Palmyra and the policies she followed in attempting to enlarge her sphere of influence.

Hellenism lay at the very center of Zenobia's cultural world. The city of Palmyra had from the early days of the Roman Empire been a bilingual city, and it is likely that it had also been in the Hellenistic period for which evidence is only now finally coming to light. But the many inscriptions we have from Palmyra from the first century down to the time of Zenobia herself show that the dialect of Aramaic current there was evenly balanced by the Greek language. It is also clear that Greek influenced Palmyrene in its diction rather more than Palmyrene influenced Greek. Furthermore the columns, the architecture, the reliefs, and the funerary portraits that abound in the physical remains of Palmyra show throughout a strong Hellenic influence. They show at the same time a distinctively oriental, or rather Palmyrene, influence that is a visual illustration of the bilingual culture we can trace in the inscriptions.

This cultural mixture was extended as well to the divine sphere, and for most of the native Palmyrene divinities we have appropriate Greek counterparts. The representation of the Palmyrene divinities also reflects the styles of Greek religion for the matching gods. The most stunning example of this is a statue that was discovered not long ago at the temple of the principal goddess of the Palmyrene pantheon, Allât. This goddess, who is the equivalent of Athena, was represented by a statue in marble that is cut in the shape of the great Athena Parthenos at Athens. It is even possible that this marble, which is not native to Syria, came itself from Greece and was cut there for export to Syria. The statue of Palmyrene Allât in the shape of Greek Athena fittingly symbolizes the world over which Zenobia presided and of which she was fiercely proud.

She gathered around her in the sumptuous buildings of the oasis city one of the most luminous collections of Greek intellectuals ever to adorn a royal salon. She brought to Palmyra the leading literary figure in the Greek culture of the time, a certain Longinus, who could well be the author of the finest piece of literary criticism to have come down to us from antiquity. The treatise known as *On the Sublime* is ascribed to an author called Longinus, whose date is unclear, but there is much to be said for believing that the great figure of Zenobia's court could have been its author.[3] In addition to that great man, Zenobia brought over an eminent literary figure from Athens, an orator by the name of Callinicus. This man happened to be another representative of Near Eastern Hellenism because he was himself a native of Petra, the great rockbound city in Roman Arabia (the modern Kingdom of Jordan); and he only later made his career in Greek literature in Greece itself. He was therefore a natural person for Zenobia to tempt to her court at Palmyra, and he had well–placed friends in the

Roman government. His treatise on bad literary style was dedicated to the governor of Arabia, Virius Lupus, who appears to have had (or at least needed) some taste in literature. Another of Callinicus's works was a history of Alexandria that he formally presented to the queen of Palmyra. Zenobia's almost fanatical devotion to Hellenic culture is no better illustrated than in her adoption of the name Cleopatra after the armies of Palmyra had taken over Egypt in the A.D. 270s. In fact, it was under the name of Cleopatra that Zenobia received from Callinicus, the Greek orator from Petra, the essay he dedicated to her on the history of the city of Alexandria.[4]

From all of this it should be clear that the support that Zenobia is alleged to have provided to a Christian leader, Paul of Samosata, did not represent an attempt to intrude Arab or oriental influences into the young Christian church in Syria. On the contrary, whatever interested her in Paul was undoubtedly the strong Hellenic character of the Christian church of Syrian Antioch. The struggles that Paul of Samosata had with various enemies within the Christian church cannot be viewed as anything other than the characteristically common internecine strife of the early church.[5] We must not fall victim to the old and dangerous habit of assuming that polar forces of Greek versus oriental were in some kind of sinister operation.

Zenobia's Hellenism was thoroughgoing, fully evident, and entirely consistent with the traditions of the city over which she ruled. The bilingual Palmyrene culture was not a culture of two worlds placed uneasily beside one another. It was one world, one common culture that was, at the same time, capable of expression in Palmyrene Aramaic and in Greek. Palmyra was no more two worlds than a truly bilingual person is two persons. For the ultimate proof of the absence of any conflict between Hellenism and the indigenous traditions at Palmyra, we can turn to the Arab traditions that survive fortunately in the historical works of early Islam.

It is odd that scholars concerned wtih Zenobia or even the emperor Aurelian have rarely thought it worthwhile to consider the substantial body of evidence about Zenobia from the Arab side. Certainly if one were even to think of a conflict between Arab and Greek, oriental and Roman, it would be necessary to see whether some reflection of this conflict appeared in the Arab sources. Arabic historiography about Zenobia is largely based on the poems of a certain Adî ibn Zaid al-'Abbâdî, whose account of Zenobia's exploits is best seen in the histories of al-Ṭabarî and al-Mas'ûdî, who represent, along with Ibn Khaldûn, the best in Islamic historiography. The character of the Arabic histories of Zenobia can be briefly stated. The Arabs viewed Zenobia's ambition, conquests, and dominions entirely in terms of an internal struggle among Arab tribes. Her defeat is ascribed to a rival Arab leader, who can be seen to have worked together with dissident elements inside of Palmyra itself. Those dissident elements, as we know from Palmyrene inscriptions, were not hostile to Zenobia because of her Hellenism.[6] On the contrary, they joined forces with Aurelian; and Aurelian joined forces with the Arab enemies.

In other words, Zenobia was removed for political reasons. She was an unacceptable usurper in Roman eyes, and she was exactly the same in Arab eyes. She posed a threat to other Arab tribes, and hence they joined against her. What is particularly remarkable in the Arabic tradition is that there is not the slightest trace of hostility to Zenobia or criticism of her for what might theoretically have been considered Hellenic excesses or affectations. The Arabs' complete lack of interest in the Greek court that Zenobia assembled for her edification can only be a compelling demonstration that the Arabs felt no tension or conflict between their own indigenous traditions and the cultural Hellenism that was deeply rooted in Syria. The Arab sources complement the Greco-Roman ones marvelously. They show the usurpation of Zenobia in its true political light while at the same time affirming the unity of Palmyrene culture within the Arab and the Roman spheres of influence.

Zenobia was no less a Hellene than Cleopatra, whose name she took for herself. When the army of Palmyra took over Egypt in A.D. 270, she saw herself as the direct successor of Cleopatra, whose family had come from Macedonia and wrested control of the land of the Pharaohs. Even before Cleopatra's martial ancestors had settled along the Nile, Thucydides had put into the mouth of Pericles the fundamental truth that has been illustrated here: Greek culture—Hellenism—is not confined to one people. Spreading out from Athens, it belongs to all those who share in the traditions of the Greeks:

> With great signs and in possession of a well attested power we shall be wondered at by those today and those to come. We need no Homer to praise us nor anyone to provide instant gratification with words, for the truth will outstrip the mere implications of our achievements. We have compelled every sea and land to lie open to our daring, and everywhere we have planted everlasting memorials of our trials no less than our triumphs.[7]

Because it was so adaptable, Hellenism was so very influential. It is good to be reminded periodically that inflexibility is not the road to success and influence. Hellenism had the unique capacity to adapt and adjust to all sorts of local traditions without losing its own recognizable identity. And for the same reason Hellenism did not eradicate the traditions with which it joined; it renewed and strengthened them. The regional identity of the communities of the Near East was more sharply defined through the prism of the Greeks, and the gods and stories of indigenous peoples acquired currency and permanence by their transmutation into Greek idioms.[8] Zenobia failed in her aspiration to dominate the lands from Syria to Egypt, but she was not opposed as an outsider by either the Romans or the Arabs. Hers was perceived by both to be an internal struggle. That she could be a Roman to the Romans and an Arab to the Arabs can only be explained by the miraculous refracting power of Hellenism.

NOTES

1. For Zenobia's property at Tivoli, *Historia Augusta, Tyr. Trig.* 30.27, together with the evidence in G. W. Bowersock, "Arabs and Sara-

cens in the *Historia Augusta,"* forthcoming in *Bonner Historia-Augusta-Colloquium,* 1984.

2. *Corpus Inscriptionum Semiticarum* 2.3971: *"corrector* of all the East," cf. 2.3946. See also G. W. Bowersock, *Roman Arabia* (1983), 130, n. 32.

3. G. Luck, "Die Schrift vom Erhabenen und ihr Verfasser," *Arctos: Acta Philologica Fennica* n.s. 5 (1967): 97–113. *Historia Augusta, Aur.* 30.3 on Longinus *quo illa* (sc. Zenobia) *magistro usa esse ad Graecas litteras dicitur* obviously does not mean, as occasionally said, that Zenobia herself was ignorant of Greek.

4. See A. Stein, "Kallinikos von Petrai," *Hermes* 58 (1923): 448–456.

5. On the whole affair, with full citation of the sources, F. Millar, "Paul of Samosata, Zenobia and Aurelian: The Church, Local Culture and Political Allegiance in Third-Century Syria," *Journal of Roman Studies* 61 (1971): 1–17.

6. The most thorough examination of Arabic texts on Zenobia will be found in M. Piotrovskii, "Arabskaya Versiya Istorii Tsaritsy Zenobii (Az-Zabby)," *Palestinskii Sbornik* 21 (1970): 170–183. For comparison with Palmyrene evidence, Bowersock, op. cit. (n. 2), 133–137.

7. Thucydides 2.41.4.

8. Interesting material on Near Eastern mosaics may be seen in *Iconographie classique et identités régionales: Bulletin de correspondance hellénique, Supplément XIV,* ed. L. Kahil, C. Augé, and P. Linant de Bellefonds (Paris, 1986). For local traditions preserved in Greek, see Pierre Chuvin, *Mythologie et géographie dans les Dionysiaques de Nonnos de Panopolis,* forthcoming.

The Reception of Greek Literature in Armenia
Robert W. Thomson

The subject of the impact of Greek literature on the Armenians is vast, covering many different genres of writing and an exceedingly long period of time. The first direct contacts between Armenians and Greeks occurred in the early fifth century B.C., when an Armenian contingent was included in the army of the great King Xerxes at the time of his invasion of Greece. But these contacts were hardly literary, and for direct influences of Greece on Armenia we have to go down to the time of Alexander the Great. In order to bring some coherence to what could be a rambling catalogue, we shall have to define a few specific themes.

Armenia played a role in the eastern Mediterranean from the time of the Old Persian Empire. After the conquests of Alexander the Great Armenia attained political independence. Plutarch in particular gives elaborate descriptions of the cultural life in Armenia in the first century B.C.—the enthusiasm of King Tigran for Greek playwrights and philosophers, and the expertise of his son, the later King Artavazd, in writing tragedies, orations, and histories in the Greek language. One could devote a whole lecture to the reception of Greek culture in the Armenia of this time; for although none of the texts written by Artavazd have survived, there are the archaeological evidence of coins, inscriptions, and buildings, and the outside literary sources on which to draw. But such cultural influences did not lead to the development of a specifically Armenian tradition of literature. So this essay is concerned with Greek influences on writings in the Armenian language. It is important to emphasize that these could not occur until the year 400 of the Christian era, when a specific script for Armenian was invented. Until then Armenians did not attempt to set down their native tongue in writing. They did not use a Greek or Aramaic alphabet for Armenian. Rather, when they needed to set up an inscription, stamp coins, or send messages, these were written in Greek or Aramaic.

Although our theme begins with the invention of a script for Armenian, this momentous invention cannot be regarded as a sudden inspiration releasing Armenia from centuries of illiteracy. It is rather the last act in a long process, that of the conversion of Armenia to Christianity. This is not the occasion to rehearse the struggle of the church in Armenia to gain a dominant position in the country after the conversion of the King Trdat (Tiridates) in A.D. 314. Even by the fifth century the war had not been won completely, for our sources stress that the invention of the alphabet was conceived as the weapon with which to effect the final conversion of the populace at large. Just as in the time of Tigran certain circles in Armenia had evinced an enthusiasm for Greek literature, so in Christian circles in the fourth century the educated classes had received training in Greek and had become familiar with Christian literature. But for the church Greek was not the only language of liturgy and study; Syrian missionaries had played an important role in bringing the gospel to Southern Armenia. So until the early fifth century both Greek and Syriac were used whenever a written text was required. To understand the history of Armenian theological and liturgical traditions this dual heritage is important to remember.

Outside the church the language of cultural aspiration was Greek. In the fourth century many Armenians went to Antioch to study under the famous teacher of rhetoric, Libanius; we know some of their names from his surviving correspondence. But Antioch was not the only city in the eastern Mediterranean frequented by Armenian students. We hear of them in

Beirut and Alexandria. In Athens the sophist Prohaeresius, who came from Persian Armenia, made a reputation for himself; and in Anatolia, the cities of Melitene, Caesarea, and Constantinople attracted Armenians. Although no schools had developed in Armenia proper, there were tutors available; the inventor of the Armenian script, who came of good family, had received a Greek education in his native province of Taron, just west of Lake Van.

We know only a little of the early life of the inventor of the Armenian script, called Mashtots or Mesrop. After his death one of his pupils, Koriun, wrote a short biography of the master. This is important as a literary document, being the first example of biographical writing in the Armenian language, and showing the influence of the Greek tradition represented by such works as the *Oration on Saint Basil* by Gregory of Nazianzus. But it is rather short on facts about the life of Mashtots at the royal chancellery before he abandoned a secular career for life as a hermit. After some years his ascetic fame attracted disciples, and with them he embarked on missionary travels to the remoter parts of the country. It was precisely for the success of this missionary work among people devoid of interest in Greek culture that Mashtots realized the importance of a script. He was anxious not only to preach orally in Armenian, but also to have the liturgy and Bible available in the native tongue. Since he was working on the Persian side of the frontier that divided Armenia unequally between the Iranian and the Roman empires, Mashtots went to the nearest center of Christian learning, Edessa, in his quest for help. Eventually a script was fashioned at Samosata with the assistance of a Greek calligrapher. We need not dwell here on the details of this script, save to note that it is modelled on Greek, not on a Semitic alphabet. In concert with the Armenian patriarch and with the encouragement of the king, Mashtots organized groups of young men who, after learning the script, went abroad to learn Syriac or Greek (or both), to collect relevant texts of an ecclesiastical stamp, and to translate these into Armenian.

We thus have reflected in a Christian context a pattern that had been established long before. But this time, instead of attending the famous pagan academies, the disciples of Mashtots went to the main centers of Christian learning; and instead of imbibing directly the rhetorical traditions of Hellenistic culture, they immersed themselves in Christian texts that had a direct bearing on the missionary work of Mashtots. Given, therefore, the long-standing interest in Greek literature shown by educated Armenian circles, and the fact that for two or three generations Armenian clerics had been familiar with Christian texts in Greek and Syriac, it is not at all surprising that within a decade or so this effort at translation bore direct fruit. Koriun compares the joy of the Armenians at having the word of God in their own tongue with the joy of the Israelites at seeing the words of God inscribed on the tablets in Hebrew. Even more important, from our present point of view, is that these students who learned Greek and Syriac and made the translations, themselves in maturer years composed the first original works in Armenian.

Equally significant is the fact that these first works in Armenian were of an ecclesiastical nature. For Armenians possessed a rich heritage of oral tales and epic songs dealing with the gods, heroes, and noteworthy figures—real or imaginary—of their past. These were recited by bards, and accompanied on the lyre or other instrument. Such musical entertainments were popular in princely circles, but these bards did not put their songs into writing. Singers of tales, like dancing girls, were frowned upon by the clergy. So, apart from a few fragments preserved by early historians or antiquarian scholars, nothing survives of a long prewritten culture that might reflect the interests and enthusiasms of the mass of the people. The written literature that developed with such remarkable rapidity in the fifth century was the perquisite of a small group, which deliberately set itself apart from pagan traditions. Armenian writing, therefore, does not give a full picture of Armenian culture, especially in the early years before pre-Christian traditions gradually faded.

Once the church in Armenia had acquired the basic liturgical, Biblical, and other necessary theological texts, the educated circles did not stop their habit of traveling abroad in search of learning and of new manuscripts to render into Armenian. Several surviving biographical documents show that Armenian scholars continued to frequent the centers of Christian learning in the eastern Mediterranean. Although some of these claims may be challenged as rhetorical exaggerations, there can be no doubt of the reverence that Armenian scholars had for Jerusalem as a center of pilgrimage, or for Constantinople as the "mother of science." However, it is noteworthy that Armenian scholars consistently sought out patristic texts of the period predating the Council of Chalcedon and the ensuing rift between the churches. There was little interest in the later development of Byzantine Greek literature.

Within a generation or two of the invention of the script their travels brought Armenians not only to Christian schools but also to participate in the more general education offered in late antiquity. Their study of philosophy, for example, began with the translation of Plato. But much more significant for the development of original Armenian works was the rendering into Armenian of various works by David, who taught in Alexandria in the second half of the sixth century. His *Definitions and Divisions of Philosophy* and his commentaries on Aristotle's *Categories* and *Analytics* and on Porphyry's *Eisagoge* formed the foundation for later Armenian works of a similar kind. For the translator did not merely render these books into Armenian, he adapted them for an Armenian audience by changing the examples used in the argument to examples which would have meaning for contemporary Armenians. In later times legends developed around the figure of this David; he was turned into an Armenian who had been a pupil of Mashtots and who had played a role in the formation of the Armenian theological position—an interesting example of a tendency to put back to the time of the inventor of the script the origin of specific Armenian traditions that had only gradually developed over the centuries.

Grammar was a topic that particularly appealed to Armenians. The *Ars Grammatica* of Dionysius Thrax was not merely translated; the text was adapted for the Armenian language, and in later generations many commentaries were composed. Textbooks of rhetoric were translated, such as the *Progymnasmata* of Theon of Alexandria, and these provided not only models of composition but also information about classical Greek literature. So it must be emphasized that the knowledge of Greek evinced by Artavazd and such persons many centuries before had no direct impact on Christian Armenia. It is the culture of the fourth, fifth, and sixth centuries of the Christian era that set the basis for Armenian literary expression.

Before turning to an examination of original Armenian works it will be helpful to cast a quick eye over some other texts translated in the early period from Greek into Armenian. Such texts provided a reservoir from which the Armenian authors could draw specific ideas or themes, and also gave models for the pattern of new works in Armenian. The most space was taken by the great Fathers of the church, John Chrysostom, Gregory of Nazianzus, Basil of Caesarea, Cyril of Alexandria, and a host of other famous names. Numerous lives of saints and martyrs provided models for the descriptions of persecutions in Armenia by Sasanian, or later Muslim, authorities. The lives and sayings of the Egyptian Fathers, popular throughout the Christian world, were a source of enjoyment and gave a pattern for the idiosyncracies of Armenian holy men and hermits. And the *Hexaemeron* of Basil of Caesarea gave readers information about the physical world and natural phenomena in a more appealing fashion than the few more technically scientific works that had been translated.

But special emphasis must be given to two works by Eusebius of Caesarea. His *Ecclesiastical History* (actually translated from the Syriac version rather than directly from the Greek original) not only provided a fund of historical information, widely quoted and adapted by Armenian writers; it offered a model for the writing of history in a Christian context, a model for the description of the working of God's providence in the present world. Even more elaborate was Eusebius' *Chronicle*.

This was the main source for Armenian knowledge of the ancient world. But it was equally important for showing how the histories of the various nations meshed with one another. Armenians were particularly interested in writing history; so they used Eusebius' *Chronicle* not only for information about the non-Armenian world, but also as a framework in which to fit the glorious past of Armenia. In the hands of a sophisticated author, such as Moses of Khoren, the *Chronicle* gave a pattern which enabled him to correlate the ancient oral traditions about the origins of the Armenian people, their earliest legendary heroes and kings, into the pattern of world history, and to demonstrate the antiquity of Armenia as a distinct and individual nation.

Armenian literature deals with Armenian themes, and over the years it developed its own traditions in matters of style, imagery, and form. But the earliest compositions do not differ in any startling way from the type of work that was being produced in the fourth and fifth centuries outside Armenia. So when Koriun wished to compose a biography of his master Mashtots, he already had in his mind some idea of how a biography should be arranged. The parallels between his work and the *Oration on Basil of Caesarea* by Gregory Nazianzus, noted above, are thus not surprising. It would be more surprising if Koriun had developed an entirely new, original style that bore no resemblance to anything that had gone before. Koriun's biography, however, did set an example in Armenian and it was used and adapted by later writers. On the other hand, a more complex composition by Eznik, one of Koriun's contemporaries and colleagues, did not set a pattern for later imitation. It may be worth looking more closely at this.

Eznik was also a disciple of Mashtots. He had traveled to Edessa and Constantinople in order to learn Syriac and Greek, and he had brought back theological texts that were significant for the Christological debates of the fifth century. But his fame today depends on a treatise dealing with the problem of the origin of evil. Eznik expounded his theme by attacking four groups who had the "wrong" interpretation of God as responsible for evil, and who did not understand correctly the Christian doctrine of man's free will. These four groups were the ancient pagan Greeks; the Persians—more precisely, the worshippers of Zurvan as the supreme god; the later Greek philosophers; and the heretical sect of Marcion. Eznik refutes one by one their false interpretations and demonstrates that there is no created thing which is evil by nature. Evil results from man's perversion of the free will given him by God. In this treatise Eznik borrows heavily from Greek writers, both Christian and pagan. The most important of his sources was the work of the Christian philosopher Methodius (died 311), whose work *On the Freedom of the Will* attacked dualism and determinism as found in the gnostic system of Valentinus. Yet Eznik's work, which has received attention both as a model of pure style and for its information about Zurvanism, did not have much influence on Armenian writers after his own time. The themes of paganism, Marcionite heresy, and Persian mythology were too closely related to the generation of Eznik and the times before him to be adaptable to the needs of later centuries. By then paganism was irrelevant, Gnostic theories had been forgotten, and Zurvanites no longer threatened. Eznik's work was not so relevant for the burning concerns of defending Christian Armenian traditions against the claims of the imperial Byzantine church or against the temptations of apostasy to Islam. It was rather the themes of the first great historians that lived on to influence succeeding generations of Armenians.

We are not here concerned with the development of Armenian literature as such, but rather with the Armenians' debt to Greek literature. But it is no chance that the author of the received history of Armenia's conversion to Christianity in the days of King Trdat calls himself by the Greek name Agathangelos, "the good messenger." He claims to be a "Roman, not unskilled in literary composition," whom the king had summoned to record the momentous events surrounding the work of Saint Gregory the Illuminator. The claim is false, because the work was composed in Armenian after the invention of the Armenian script.

The reference to Agathangelos as coming from Rome is deliberate, since the author emphasizes the concordat between the newly converted Emperor Constantine and the newly converted Armenian King Trdat which was supposedly ratified in that city. However, Rome in Italy was not a source for Armenian learning and scholarship. Rather it was to the New Rome, Constantinople, that Armenians traveled in large numbers, and it was to Greek, not Latin, sources that they were indebted. The respect given Constantinople may be inferred from a reference in the work of the late fifth-century historian Lazar of Parp. He refers to an earlier Armenian history attributed to a certain Faustos, of whom nothing is known. Faustos's work bore the title *Buzandaran,* which means a collection of heroic tales. But Lazar, and others after him, confused this with Byzantium, and since Lazar disapproved of the pagan tone of Faustos, he refused to believe that such an author could hail from Byzantium, "the nurse of the sciences." Constantinople is also praised by the more famous Moses of Khoren, who claims to have visited the capital himself. Describing the building of the city by Constantine, he speaks of Byzantium as a city from which streams of wisdom flow out into all parts of the world.

We should linger for a moment on the *History of Armenia* by this Moses of Khoren. It had a greater influence on later Armenian historical writing than any other work, since it was the first and most successful attempt to describe the origins of the Armenian people. Moses was one of the most widely read of the early Armenian authors. Although he rarely identifies his sources, it can be shown that he borrowed from many Greek texts. The interesting point is that Moses did not take his fragmentary knowledge of the classical world directly from the ancient Greek authors, despite the fact that he wishes to convey that impression by omitting the intermediary source. It was the *Chronicle* of Eusebius, the *Alexander Romance,* the *Progymnasmata* of Theon, the *Scholia* of Nonnus, and works by Philo of Alexandria that provided him with knowledge of classical myths and of Homer. He did not read the *Iliad* or *Odyssey* in the original, nor are any Armenian translations of these poems known until the eighteenth century.

Another text written in Greek had a profound effect on Moses, both as a source for information and as a model for the Armenian situation. This was the *Jewish Wars* by Josephus. He takes many passages which refer to the Roman–Parthian wars in which the Armenians played a role, and distorts them to enhance the significance of the Armenian kings Tigran and Artavazd. Details of these borrowings do not concern us here, but we should note the specific parallel he draws between the Jews and the Armenians. For, just as Josephus at the beginning of the *Jewish Wars* reprimands the Greeks for ignoring the exploits of a small people, so Moses emphasizes that Armenia, "a small country, restricted in numbers, weak in power, and often subject to another's rule," has nonetheless produced its own heroes who accomplished many deeds worthy of being recorded.

Moses is the first Armenian writer to give an explicit philosophy of historical writing. Its purpose is to bequeath a record to posterity, but not everything that happened in the past is worthy of record: only the deeds of great men, both heroic exploits and notable acts of wise government. Moses does not suggest that there is any didactic purpose in historiography. Without denying God's general providence and protection of the world, he does not hold up lessons of moral conduct to remind his readers of the ultimate fate that befalls the wicked. But, according to Moses, a historian does have responsibilities. These may be summarized as veracity, elegance, and strict chronology. These themes are taken from the textbooks of rhetoric known to Moses and his contemporaries, of which the Armenian version of Theon's *Progymnasmata* was the most influential.

Moses' references to his foreign travels, and the clear evidence of texts of rhetoric used in the contemporary schools of the eastern Mediterranean, bring us to a unique figure in early Armenian scholarship and to an unusual document. Anania of Shirak, who lived in the seventh century, is the first Armenian to have devoted his attention primarily to mathematics and scientific subjects. His books on mathematics were used as textbooks in succeeding generations, while his ability in astronomy led to his being asked by the patriarch Anastasius (662–667) to establish a fixed calendar. He also wrote a *Chronicle*—the first in Armenian of a continuing series of such works where significant events were listed in order under the years of their occurrence—and some theological works. Anania was a rarity in early Armenia, a lay scholar, but he was certainly familiar with patristic works, and used Basil's *Hexaemeron* as a source for some of his ideas on the nature of the heavens. The unusual document is a brief autobiography. He claims that he could find no teacher of mathematics in Armenia, so he made his way as far as Constantinople. There he heard of a teacher in Trebizond, Tychikos, with whom he studied for eight years. Returning to Armenia in order to practice his skills, Anania complains in rather petulant terms of the lack of interest shown in mathematics by his fellow-countrymen.

Despite the fact that many Armenians traveled to Constantinople and other centers of Greek learning, translated texts of various kinds, and adapted Greek writings to the Armenian situation, there was always an ambiguity in their attitude toward the Greek world. Just as the Armenian clergy ignored the pagan past of their country, so Armenian authors in general paid little direct attention to the literature of classical Greece, depending primarily on Christian sources or the handbooks of late antiquity. And although Constantinople may have appeared as a haven of learning toward which all scholars aspired, at the same time the Byzantine empire appeared as a perpetual threat to Armenian autonomy, both political and cultural. Armenian writers lay special emphasis on the threat to Armenian religious traditions. In the time of the emperor Maurice, when Armenia was divided between Iran and Byzantium and the Greeks were putting pressure on the patriarch Moses II to accept union with the imperial Church, the latter is credited with a famous retort: "I shall not cross the Azat; I shall not eat bread from the oven; I shall not drink hot water." The Azat is a tributary of the river Araxes, which marked the temporary division of the Byzantine and Iranian sectors, but the use of the word here is a pun, for in Armenian it means "free." The other two references are to the liturgy; for the Armenians did not use leavened bread or mix warm water with the wine for communion.

The pattern of jealous preservation of Armenian cultural autonomy had been emphasized earlier in a description of encroachments by a hostile power, this time from the Iranian side. So before elaborating on Armenian views of Byzantium, let us make a brief digression. For the Armenians were caught between two worlds, and their relationship to danger from one side influenced their attitude to danger from the other.

In A.D. 450 most of Armenia formed a province of the Sasanian Empire. In protest at the suppression of traditional liberties during the reign of the Shah Yazkert II (439–457) the Armenians rose in revolt. Strongly supported by the leaders of the church, Prince Vardan Mamikonean faced the Persians at the battle of Avarayr in 451. He was killed, and the leaders, both lay and cleric, of the defeated Armenians were taken to Khorasan as prisoners. The events of these two years, and the survivors' final release from captivity, were described in one of the most famous and influential works of early Armenian literature, the *History of Vardan and the Armenian War* by Elishe. What gives this work its preeminent status is not the narrative of events, which were also recorded by other Armenian authors, but rather Elishe's interpretation of those events in general terms, so that later generations could adapt them for their own times and altered circumstances. He saw the war of 450–451 as a struggle between vice and virtue in which the Armenians were fighting for their ancestral customs: Death in that cause is more honorable than life with ignominy; the true patriot is the defender of Christianity against Zoroastrianism; apostasy not only leads to personal damnation, it brings about the ruin of the people. Elishe's basic themes are the covenant of loyalty to church and country, and the valor of the virtuous as contrasted with the cowardice and baseness of those who abandoned that covenant.

One source, written mostly in Greek but not Greek in a narrower sense, had a particular influence on this *History of Vardan:* the books of Maccabees. Although other Armenian historians had used the books of Maccabees and had seen comparisons with the situation of the Armenians, more than any other writer Elishe adapts the Maccabees' situation to his own. The Persians take the place of the Seleucids, Shah Yazkert is depicted in the same terms as King Antiochus, while the idea of death for ancestral traditions is modeled on a basic theme of the books of the Maccabees. From Elishe on, Armenian writers were able to draw on powerful symbols of constancy to an ideal both religious and national that stirred a responsive chord in their readers' hearts. Elishe's classic work also draws attention to a feature of Armenian cultural life that was of relevance to their attitude toward Byzantium. The clergy, concerned with the preservation of Christian values, was strongly influenced by Greek traditions and looked to Constantinople for help. The nobles, however, were strongly imbued with Iranian traditions, and many of them had more sympathy for the cultural life of the Sasanian Empire than for the foreign, city-oriented, culture of the Greco-Roman world. After all, for 1,000 years Armenia had formed part of the greater Iranian world; it was misleading for Elishe to claim that long-standing traditional values had been Christian ones, since the new religion was still struggling at the beginning of the fifth century for the support of the mass of the people; and the church itself was organized along the pattern of the great noble families, not that of the political administration of the Roman Empire.

If we turn back to the question of Armenian reception of Greek literature it is now easier to understand the attitude of later generations toward the literature of Byzantium. We have already noted the number of translations into Armenian made of patristic works, of Greek philosophers and rhetoricians, and of Jewish works by Josephus and Philo. There was also a good deal of translation from Syriac into Armenian, but again of Christian and early writers. However, of texts written in Byzantium after the final break between the churches in the sixth century, only the *Hexaemeron* by George of Pisidia (seventh century), various theological letters sent to Armenia by Greek patriarchs, and a late translation of works by John of

Damascus and John Climachus can be identified. This does not mean that nothing Byzantine was read, for the Armenian chroniclers were clearly familiar with events in Byzantine history. But it does mean that most Armenian scholars and writers were not interested in contemporary Greek writers. For example, when the scholar Stephen, later bishop of the province of Siunik in eastern Armenia, was in Constantinople in the second decade of the eighth century, he set his hand to translating works by Gregory of Nyssa and Dionysius the Areopagite. One looks in vain for Armenian versions of Procopius, Agathias, Theophanes, Psellus, Anna Comnena, or other notable Byzantine writers. And despite the wealth of information about Byzantine politics and military history to be found in Armenian sources, there are practically no references to Byzantine authors, either as models to be emulated or as texts to be consulted.

Yet, as emphasized earlier, Armenia was never a monolithic whole. Just as in earlier days there had been tension between those who looked to the Greek world and those who were locked firmly in the grip of Iranian culture, so in later centuries there was tension between admirers of Greek Christian traditions and those who adhered to Armenian individuality. The most extreme example of philhellenism is provided by the eleventh-century scholar and man of affairs, Gregory Magistros.

Over the centuries many Armenians had given service in the Byzantine government or the army. Many had risen to positions of eminence, and some had attained the imperial throne after a generation or two of acculturation. Such Armenians were integrated into the ethnically diverse population of the empire, had accepted the authority of the Greek church, and were more or less lost to Armenia in the sense that their careers had little direct influence on the cultural life of their native land. The career of Gregory Magistros is thus unusual for although he served as duke of southwestern Armenia for the imperial government after 1048, he pursued his literary activity in the Armenian language. His interests were primarily philosophical: he translated works of Plato and Euclid, wrote a commentary on the *Grammar* of Dionysius Thrax (which had earlier been translated into Armenian), and wrote a series of letters on scholarly and administrative matters. These letters are unique in Armenian, being not only personal communications as opposed to official documents, but also unique in style. Gregory Magistros had spent some years in Constantinople and was deeply imbued with the contemporary Greek enthusiasm for classical learning. His letters abound in recondite allusions to the literature of pagan antiquity; and their tortuous language, rich in neologisms, reflects the rhetorical obscurity of Byzantine style. However, his literary work lies outside the mainstream of Armenian cultural activity. Later generations did not follow his enthusiasm for Byzantine secular learning, and no one imitated his epistolary style.

My purpose has been to illustrate the importance of written Greek sources in the development of Armenian literature, and to hint at the ambivalent attitude of Armenians to the contemporary culture of Byzantium. In one essay it would be impossible to cover the literary history of 1,000 years, or even to list the Greek texts which had an impact in Armenia, let alone to chart the troubled course of Armenian-Greek relations in a wider sense. However, a few general points may serve as a conclusion:

1. The influence of pagan Greek literature in pre-Christian Armenia had no discernible effect on the later development of Armenian literature.

2. Armenian literature begins after the year A.D. 400 in a Christian context.

3. The Greek texts that helped to shape Armenian literature were primarily ecclesiastical.

4. The nonecclesiastical texts to which Armenians were indebted for their knowledge of secular and technical subjects were those of late antiquity, not the classics of ancient Greece.

5. Once an individual Armenian literary tradition had developed, Armenians became less interested in contemporary Greek writing, even though they continued to seek out earlier Greek patristic texts.

Earlier we noted that Armenian writers thought of Constantinople as the source of wisdom. It would be appropriate to end with their reaction to the fall of the city to the Turks. For, despite all the animosities and hatreds during the intervening millennium, Armenians did regard the end of Byzantium as a grievous blow. There exist several elegies devoted to this theme. Abraham of Ancyra was an eyewitness, and he thinks of the capture of Constantinople in terms of God's punishment for the Greeks' lack of piety and the Latins' intolerance. On the other hand, Arakel from Bitlis, near Lake Van, was not present and does not regard the fall of the city as the end of Christian civilization. Before his time there had developed in Armenia a genre of apocalyptic and prophetic writings, but these had been restricted to Armenian themes, predicting the eventual restoration of particular dynasties or successions of patriarchs. Arakel connects such ideas with a grander world outlook. Harking back to the old theme of the alliance between the Emperor Constantine and the newly converted King Tiridates, Arakel predicts that Constantinople, the herald of God's kingdom on earth and chosen by God as the city of saints, will be recovered and that Jerusalem will be reconquered by Frankish armies from the West. And those Frankish armies of deliverance will be led by Armenian soldiers descended from those who accompanied King Tiridates to Rome and were kept there by Constantine. Not only will Constantinople and Jerusalem be recovered, but the ancient Arsacid dynasty to which Tiridates belonged will be restored, and the patriarchal line of Saint Gregory the Illuminator will return.

For Arakel these events were closely connected with contemporary questions of Armenian history. Only eleven years before the fall of Constantinople the seat of the Armenian patriarchs had been restored to the ancient site of Ejmiatsin in northeastern Armenia, which had always been associated with Saint Gregory. And if the patriarchal line had been restored, perhaps deliverance from the oppressive Muslim yoke would not be far behind. Arakel's hopeful predictions illustrate the ever-present admiration of Armenians for Greek culture, which was never totally obscured by political and religious differences.

The Byzantine Missions of Saints Cyril and Methodius
Dimitri Obolensky

The ninth century was, for the Byzantine Empire, a period of political revival and cultural expansion. This recovery was marked by four principal events: the removal of the Arab threat from the eastern frontier; the defeat of Iconoclasm, which ended a century-long crisis that had split the Byzantine church and society, and gravely crippled the empire's foreign policy; the revival of secular education; and the resurgence of the missionary energies of the Byzantine church. This essay is concerned with the last of these topics and with two men who embody, in religious and cultural activity, some of the most vital forces which, in the middle of the ninth century, combined to inaugurate what the foremost Byzantinist of our time, George Ostrogorsky, called the "Golden Age of the Byzantine Empire."

The two men, Constantine and Methodius, were two brothers from Thessalonica. In my opinion, they were Greeks, insofar as this term can be meaningfully applied to ninth-century Byzantines; the efforts of some historians to prove that they were wholly or partly Slav by birth seem misguided. They came from a family with a tradition of public service. Methodius, the elder brother, held for a while a high administrative post in one of the Slav provinces of the Byzantine Empire. Constantine (later to be known under his monastic name of Cyril) was given an extensive education in Constantinople in the 840s. He studied philosophy, geometry, and dialectics at the feet of the two greatest scholars of the age, Leo the Mathematician and

Photius, the future patriarch. Both brothers early experienced a call to the religious life. Methodius became a monk in the great monastic foundation of Mount Olympus in western Asia Minor; Constantine, who remained in the Byzantine capital, was ordained deacon or priest (which of the two we do not know for certain) and appointed to a chair at the University of Constantinople.

Most of our knowledge of their lives comes from their Slavonic biographies, known to scholars today as the *Vita Constantini* and the *Vita Methodii*.[1] The *Vita Constantini* was written within thirteen years of Constantine-Cyril's death, and the *Vita Methodii* was composed soon after Methodius' death in 885. They are thus to all intents and purposes contemporary biographies. Their authenticity and reliability were demonstrated in a seminal book published in Prague in 1933. Its author, Father Dvornik, was able to show how accurately the biographies reflect the intellectual climate of ninth-century Byzantium.[2] An English translation of both was published in 1976 by the University of Michigan.[3]

The *Vita Constantini* tells at some length of the first diplomatic mission carried out by Constantine, probably in 851. At the age of twenty-four, he took part in an embassy to the court of the Arab Khalife. His medieval biographer presents this embassy as a theological disputation between Constantine and teachers of Islam. It is perhaps more likely that its main purpose was to persuade the Khalife to rescind a number of edicts he had recently published, restricting the movement of his Christian subjects. From the Byzantine point of view, the embassy seems to have been a failure.

The next diplomatic mission with which Constantine was entrusted by the Byzantine government was to the ruler of the Khazars north of the Caucasus. This time, in 860, he was apparently appointed chief ambassador and took Methodius with him. Here too his biographer is chiefly interested in the doctrinal disputations which Constantine held with Jewish rabbis, whose influence was powerful at the Khazar court. It is probable, however, that the mission had a political purpose:

to confirm the traditional alliance between Byzantium and the Khazars, in the face of the common danger from the Viking Russians. On the religious plane Constantine's embassy achieved little: the Khazar ruling classes had, it seems, already embraced Judaism. Politically, it was more successful, and the Khazar alliance with the empire was reaffirmed.

During both these embassies Constantine showed himself a firm believer in the basic tenet of Byzantine political philosophy: the concept of the one universal Christian empire, the pattern and prefiguration on earth of the kingdom of God. "All the arts," he proudly declared to the Arabs, "have come from us."[4] And to the Khazars he said, more explicitly still: "Our Empire is . . . that of Christ, as the prophet has said, 'The God of heaven shall set up a kingdom, which shall never be destroyed: and the kingdom shall not be left to other people, but it shall break in pieces and consume all these kingdoms, and it shall stand for ever.'"[5]

The third and last of Constantine's embassies was to prove of far greater importance in the history of Europe than the first two. This last mission, in which he was intimately associated with his brother Methodius, will be the subject of this essay.

In 862 an embassy arrived in Constantinople: it was sent to the emperor Michael III by a Slav ruler in Central Europe, the Moravian prince Rastislav. The purpose of this embassy was twofold: first, the Moravians, whose realm comprised what is today Czechoslovakia and western Hungary, were hard pressed by their neighbors, the Franks and the Bulgarians, and wished to conclude a political alliance with Byzantium. The second aim of the embassy was destined to be, in the long run, of far greater importance. It was to request the emperor to send the Moravians a Christian missionary acquainted with the Slavonic language. Christianity had spread to Moravia during the first half of the ninth century, but its preachers were German missionaries from Salzburg and Passau. Rastislav feared that they would threaten the precarious independence he had recently wrested from his overlord, Louis the German, King of Bavaria. A Slav-speaking clergy from Byzantium, he hoped, would help him safeguard his country's cultural autonomy.

Constantine and Methodius were the obvious choice to lead the Byzantine embassy to Moravia. Distinguished in the service of church and state, experienced diplomats, they had the added advantage of knowing the Slavonic language. Thessalonica, their native town, was a bilingual city in a Slav-speaking countryside. Methodius' biographer tells us that the emperor, in urging him and his brother to go to Moravia, argued, "You are both natives of Thessalonica, and all Thessalonians speak pure Slav."[6]

Before leaving Constantinople, Constantine invented an alphabet for the use of the Moravian Slavs. This invention was not an instantaneous affair; chief among his collaborators in his task was Methodius. Constantine's alphabet, known today as Glagolitic, was adapted to a Slav dialect of southern Macedonia, from the neighborhood of Thessalonica. With the help of his new alphabet, he translated a selection of lessons from the Gospels, intended for liturgical use.[7] In the Byzantine church the lectionary begins with the opening verses of Saint John's Gospel, which are read during the Easter liturgy: "In the beginning was the Word, and the Word was with God, and the Word was God." The gospels' symbolic relevance to the task of evangelizing the Slavs in their own language, we may be sure, was lost neither on Constantine nor on his medieval biographer.

When, in the autumn of 863, the Byzantine mission arrived in Moravia, Constantine translated (rapidly, we are told by his biographer) the Byzantine liturgical offices into the Slav language. Thus was created a new literary language, based on the spoken dialect of the Macedonian Slavs, modelled on Greek, and—because the different Slavonic languages were similar in structure and vocabulary—intelligible to all the Slavs. This literary language is known to modern scholars as Old Church Slavonic. In time its range was broadened and its vocabulary enriched by further translations of the Christian Scripture, of Greek patristic writings, and of Byzantine legal texts, as well as by the composition of original works. Old Church Slavonic became, after Greek and Latin, the third international language of Europe and the common literary idiom of those East European peoples—the Bulgarians, the Serbs, the Russians, and the

Rumanians—who gained entry into the Byzantine cultural commonwealth. Constantine, with his brother Methodius, was thus the founder of a cultural tradition, Greek in form and Slavonic in content, which was to provide a channel of great efficacy for the transmission of Byzantine culture to the medieval peoples of eastern Europe.

It was of great importance to the history of the Cyrillo–Methodian mission to the Slavs that the mission was carried out in an atmosphere of intense struggle. Constantine–Cyril and Methodius, as well as their leading disciples, became perforce fighters for a cause that had to be defended by sustained and powerful argument. They had come to Moravia at the express request of that country's authorities, but Moravia belonged to western Christendom, and to this land the Byzantines could make no convincing claim. Two further difficulties stood in the way of the Cyrillo–Methodian mission. The Frankish clergy, who had worked in Moravia for at least the past half-century, regarded these new-fangled missionaries, not without reason, as trespassers on their own missionary preserve. Furthermore these Greeks from Byzantium were engaged in a linguistic and liturgical experiment which seemed to the Franks a dangerous, indeed heretical, innovation: they celebrated the divine office not in Latin, as the custom of the western church commanded, but in Slavonic. And so, from the very onset of their mission, Constantine and Methodius were plagued by Frankish suspicion and hostility.

In the circumstances there was only one European power capable of supporting the Cyrillo–Methodian mission effectively: the Papacy, in whose overall jurisdiction Moravia lay. Four years after their arrival in that country, Constantine and Methodius traveled to Rome, in response to a summons from Pope Nicholas I. To understand the events that followed, we must bear one essential fact in mind. In the ninth century, and indeed for some considerable time to come, the Greek and the Roman churches, despite growing rivalry and doctrinal and liturgical disputes, were still a single body; a consciousness of a united Christendom had as yet forsaken neither. For most

Byzantines of the time, Rome remained the venerable city of Peter and Paul, and in its bishop, the Patriarch of the West — the "Apostolicus" as he is called in the *Vita Constantini* and the *Vita Methodii* — was vested the primacy of honor in the whole of Christendom. It is important to recognize that the attitude of Constantine and Methodius to Rome and its bishop in no way differed from that of the majority of their Byzantine compatriots.

In Rome they were received by the new pope, Hadrian II. In a decision that broke for a while the liturgical monopoly of Latin in the western church, he solemnly authorized the use of the Slavonic liturgy.

At this crucial moment in the mission's history Constantine fell seriously ill. Feeling the approach of death, he became a monk under his now more familiar name of Cyril. In 869 he died in Rome and, at his brother's request, was buried in the Church of San Clemente. His last words to his brother were to implore Methodius not to abandon their common work for the Slavs, even if it meant never returning to the monastery of Mount Olympus, where Methodius had received the tonsure. This injunction, recorded by Methodius's ninth-century biographer, provides a moving illustration of the tension we find so often in the history of the church between the missionary calling and the contemplative life: "Behold, my brother, we were both harnessed to the same yoke, ploughing the same furrow. I am falling down on the field, my day's work finished; but you have a great love of the Mountain. Do not, for the sake of the Mountain, abandon your teaching. For how better can you be saved?"[8]

The rest of Methodius' life was spent in obedience to his brother's last wish. Armed with the pope's approval of the Slavonic liturgy, he returned to central Europe, where, as archbishop of Pannonia and papal legate to the Slav nations, he continued the work of building a vernacular Christianity, translating the remaining parts of the Scriptures and training the next generation of Slav-speaking priests. But the east Frankish clergy, whose earlier prerogatives in central Europe had been annulled by Methodius' appointment by the pope, struck again. Taking advantage of the dethronement of Rastislav of Moravia by his nephew Svatopluk, who promptly acknowledged the suzerainty of Louis the German, they secured Methodius' arrest. For two and a half years Methodius was imprisoned in Swabia. In 873 the new pope, John VIII, having learned at last of his legate's plight, forced Louis the German and the Bavarian bishops to release him.

But Rome was losing interest in the Slavonic liturgy. The Papacy was now showing a growing unwillingness to risk, for the sake of this liturgy, a major conflict with the Frankish church. John VIII still loyally supported Methodius, but his successors, turning their back on the policy of Nicholas I and Hadrian II, banned the Slavonic liturgy. In 885 Methodius died in Moravia, his work among the Slavs on the brink of ruin. His principal disciples were arrested and exiled from Moravia; others were sold into slavery.

The later history of the Cyrillo–Methodian mission to the Slavs lies outside the scope of this essay. We should note, however, that at the very moment when the work of the two brothers in central Europe seemed to have utterly collapsed, a great future suddenly opened before it. Expelled from Moravia on their master's death, the disciples of Methodius found refuge in another land. Their work was saved for Europe and the Slavs by the Bulgarians, who further enriched the vernacular tradition and, in the fullness of time, transmitted it to other peoples of eastern Europe who belonged to the Byzantine cultural commonwealth. Clement, the chief disciple of Cyril and Methodius who, following his expulsion from Moravia, worked among the Macedonian Slavs for thirty years, and his companion Naum continued their masters' work in Bulgaria at the turn of the ninth century, preaching in the Slav language, celebrating the Slavonic liturgy according to the Byzantine rite, translating Greek religious writings with the help of the newly invented Cyrillic alphabet, and training a native clergy.[9]

In considering the cultural significance of the Cyrillo–Methodian mission, I pose two questions: What was the atti-

Saints Cyril and Methodius

tude of the Byzantine authorities and public opinion toward this mission? And how did the Slavs of the Middle Ages react to this Byzantine mission, whose beneficiaries they were?

There is no doubt that the aims of the Moravian mission were fully in accord with the foreign policy of the ninth-century Byzantine emperors Michael III and Basil I. They were vitally interested in the Slav world that lay beyond the empire's northern border, and were more than willing to harness for this purpose the missionary energies and experience of the church. Its missionary activity, linked more closely than ever to the aims of imperial diplomacy, was then embarking on a period of unsurpassed vigor. The 860s were for Byzantium a period of astonishing achievement. In this single decade Constantine and Methodius were sent to Moravia; Bulgaria was converted to the Christian faith; the evangelization of the Serbs was begun; and the Patriarch Photius, organizer of all these missions, announced in 867 that the Russians had abandoned paganism and accepted a bishop from Constantinople. The Slav vernacular liturgy was clearly an instrument of great efficacy in these missionary enterprises. The Byzantines, moreover, citizens of an empire that claimed to be universal, recognized in principle the right of every nation to celebrate the divine office in its own tongue. They did not forget that Saint John Chrysostom, in a sermon preached in Constantinople, had expressed his joy at the fact that the city's Gothic community chanted the liturgy in its own language: "The teaching of fishermen and tentmakers," he triumphantly announced, "shines in the language of the barbarians more brightly than the sun."[10]

Yet when all has been said in praise of the Byzantines for their willingness to admit non-Greek languages into the company of sacred liturgical tongues, it must be conceded that there is another side to the picture. The Byzantines never wholly lost the mental attitude, inherited from the ancient Greeks, which associated the notion of "barbarian" with alien tongues, and regarded them as evil-sounding and incomprehensible. They took for granted that Greek was inherently superior to all other languages. Even Latin incurred the scorn of linguistic purists.

Thus in the early thirteenth century Michael Choniates, the learned metropolitan of Athens, declared that donkeys would sooner perceive the sound of the lyre, and dung-beetles perfume, than the Latins apprehend the harmony and grace of the Greek language.[11]

This attitude about non-Greek languages must have made it difficult for some of the compatriots of Cyril and Methodius to approve of their championship of the Slavonic tongue. The *Vita Constantini* hints that when the Slav alphabet was invented some influential persons in Constantinople disapproved of this linguistic and liturgical experiment: the Emperor Michael, we are told, considered the translation of the liturgy into a foreign language as a departure from recent tradition, and Constantine himself feared that in putting his invention to practical use, he might be accused of heresy.[12]

It seems therefore that in Byzantine society, at least in the ninth and tenth centuries, there existed two contrary attitudes to the Slavonic liturgy. Its champions, who were drawn from government circles and the higher ranks of the ecclesiastical hierarchy, regarded the Slavonic vernacular tradition as a useful instrument of imperial diplomacy, as well as a reminder that in the Christian dispensation all languages are equally acceptable in the sight of the Lord. Their opponents, who belonged to the more conservative circles of the metropolitan and provincial clergy, were probably motivated partly by the conviction that Greek was superior to all other languages, and partly by professional jealousy and exclusiveness: the Slavonic liturgy endangered their liturgical monopoly and added to the practical difficulty of missionary work. It seems that this ambivalent attitude toward the Cyrillo–Methodian mission reflected a tension between the Greek classical tradition and the doctrines of Christianity which was never wholly resolved in Byzantine society.

The Cyrillo–Methodian mission was born and developed in an atmosphere of struggle. The two brothers and their disciples were forced to defend their lifework against the enemies of the Slav vernacular tradition and these were not confined to the

Franks. Furthermore they needed to explain and justify their heritage to its direct beneficiaries, the Slav peoples. This is why we find, in the writings of their followers in Moravia, Bulgaria, and Russia, so great an abundance of arguments, counter-arguments, apologies, and justifications.

In Venice in 867, on their way to Rome, Constantine and Methodius had their second encounter with an organized group of Latin clerics strongly opposed to the Slavonic liturgy. Constantine was obliged to refute their central argument, that it is permissible to celebrate the divine office only in three languages — Hebrew, Greek, and Latin — a view he branded as "the trilingual heresy." According to the *Vita Constantini,* he met their attacks with two arguments: the first was drawn from historical precedent, the second from Scripture. He cited a list of peoples who, in his words, "gave glory to God each in its own language." This list includes Armenians, Georgians, Persians, Goths, and Arabs. But the heaviest artillery he moved against the Venetian trilingualists was his citation of virtually the entire fourteenth chapter of Saint Paul's Epistle to the Corinthians. Here are some telling passages: "If the trumpet give an uncertain sound, who shall prepare himself to the battle? So likewise ye, except ye utter by the tongue words easy to be understood, how shall it be known what is spoken? For ye shall speak into the air . . . For if I pray in an unknown tongue, my spirit prayeth, but my understanding is unfruitful . . . Yet in church I had rather speak five words with my understanding, that by my voice I might teach others also, than ten thousand words in an unknown tongue."[13]

It matters little, for our present purpose, that Constantine and his biographer were quoting Saint Paul out of context, and that 1 Cor. 14 has nothing whatever to do with vernacular languages. Saint Paul is saying that "speaking in tongues," that is making ecstatic utterance, is less useful to the Christian community than rational and coherent preaching. It remains true, however, that 1 Cor. 14, with its strong emphasis on verbal intelligibility, became an ideological manifesto for more than one writer of the Cyrillo–Methodian school.

A second example of Cyrillo–Methodian apologetics may be described as an ethnic ideology, whose different elements lie scattered through many writings of that school. Central to this ideology is the belief that, by acquiring the Scriptures and the liturgy in their own language, the Slavs entered a chosen and privileged society, within which every nation had its own peculiar gifts and every people its legitimate calling. Their language had now acquired a sacramental character; and the nations who spoke it were, in turn, held to be raised to the status of a "peculiar," consecrated people. The idea of a consecrated nation is combined with that of a plurality of languages equal in status, and the incipient nationalism of the countries of eastern Europe is tempered and sublimated by what would be called today an ecumenical outlook. The Slavs, in the contest of this thought-world, regarded themselves as "a new people," λαὸς καινός, or *novyi yazyk* in their language. They were not inferior in status for being late arrivals into the community of Christian peoples. Rather they were to be regarded in the light of the parable in Saint Matthew's Gospel (20:1–16) of the householder who went out early in the morning to hire laborers to work in his vineyard: those who were hired at the eleventh hour received the same salary as those who from the beginning "had borne the burden and heat of the day." This parable is pointedly referred to by many writers of the Cyrillo–Methodian school.[14]

The third example of Cyrillo–Methodian scriptural exegesis marks an attempt to interpret the work of Cyril and Methodius within the context of the history of human salvation. The claims for this heritage now become still more ambitious.

The *Vita Methodii* cited, in an adapted Slavonic translation, the letter written in 869 by Pope Hadrian II to the Slav princes of central Europe. In this letter, which begins with the words "Glory to God in the highest, on earth peace, good-will toward men," the pope announces the appointment as his legate, and authorizes the use of the Slavonic liturgy in the lands of these princes. And he adds, as a justification for his action, "that the word of the Scriptures might be fulfilled: 'Praise the Lord, all ye nations,' and: 'All the different tongues shall tell the mighty works of God, as the Holy Spirit will give them utterance.'"[15] The second of these quotations is taken, almost verbatim, from the second chapter of the Acts of the Apostles, verses 4 and 11, which describe the descent of tongues of fire upon the apostles at Pentecost. And it clearly implies that the pope and the author of the *Vita Methodii* believed that the advent of the Slavonic liturgy and vernacular Scriptures was equivalent to a second Pentecost. The same parallel is drawn, at least implicitly, in other works of the Cyrillo–Methodian tradition.

The belief that the Slavs, provided with the liturgy and Scriptures in their own language, have entered an elitist society, and the further claim that this vernacular Christianity has its place in the economy of man's salvation, could be taken yet a step further. This step was taken by several medieval authors who, whether by citing a particular Biblical text or of their own accord, saw in the Cyrillo–Methodian heritage an element in the transfiguration of the world through the advent of the kingdom of God. And in this claim, however extravagant it may sound when put in these abstract terms, lies my fourth and last example.

Something of the kind seems to be implied in an Old Church Slavonic poem of the ninth century, the *Prologue* (*Proglas*) to the translated Gospels. Its theme is the glorification of vernacular writing and the sacred right of the Slavs—and indeed of all peoples—to possess Scriptures in their own language. The late Roman Jakobson, the leading authority of our time on the Cyrillo–Methodian tradition, ascribed the *Prologue* to Constantine–Cyril himself, and called it "an unmatched classic of Slavic homiletic poetry."[16] The author of this poem laments the fate of those without sacred books in their own language, and suggests that the Word, the *logos* the Slavs are now able to hear, can transfigure man's every sense. Here is Roman Jakobson's translation of the passage:

> As without light there can be no joy—
> For while the eye sees all of God's creation,
> Still what is seen without light lacks beauty—

> So it is with every soul lacking letters,
> And ignorant even of God's law . . .
> The law that reveals God's paradise.
> For what ear, having heard
> The sound of thunder, is not gripped with the fear of God?
> Or how can nostrils which smell no flower
> Sense the divine miracle?
> And the mouth which tastes no sweetness
> Makes of man a stone.
> Even more, the soul lacking letters
> Grows dead in human beings.

The sense of triumph and joy in the newly acquired Slavonic letters, which touch so many early medieval writings of the Cyrillo–Methodian school with the excitement of a cultural spring-time, are conveyed most powerfully in another biblical text from which the authors of the *Prologue,* of the *Vita Constantini,* and of the Russian Primary Chronicle quoted to describe the bounty of the Slav vernacular tradition. This text is found in the opening verses of the thirty-fifth chapter of the book of the prophet Isaiah, in the Septuagint version:

> The wilderness and the dry land shall be glad, the desert shall rejoice and blossom; like the crocus it shall blossom abundantly, and rejoice with joy and singing . . . Then the eyes of the blind shall be opened, and the ears of the deaf shall be unstopped. Then shall the lame man leap like a hart, and the tongue of the dumb shall be clearly heard . . . They shall see the glory of the Lord, the splendour of our God.

NOTES

1. Published in *Constantinus et Methodius Thessalonicenses. Fontes,* ed. F. Grivec and F. Tomšić (Zagreb, 1960).
2. F. Dvornik, *Les Légendes de Constantin et de Méthode vues de Byzance* (Prague, 1933).
3. "The Vita of Constantine and the 'Vita' of Methodius," transl. with commentaries by M. Kantor and R. S. White, *Michigan Slavic Materials,* no. 13 (1976): see also the English translation by S. Nikolov in

"Kiril and Methodius: Founders of Slavonic Writing," *East European Monographs* 172 (Boulder, 1985): 49–92, where the two *Vitae* are attributed, on quite inadequate evidence, to Clement of Ohrid. Cf. the French translation by A. Vaillant, *Textes vieux-slaves,* 2 (Paris, 1968): 1–25, 34–43.

    4. *Vita Constantini* (hereafter VC), ch. 6.
    5. Ibid., ch. 10.
    6. *Vita Methodii* (hereafter VM), ch. 6.
    7. VC, ch. 14.
    8. VM, ch. 7.
    9. See *Monumenta ad SS Cyrilli et Methodii successorum vitas resque gestas pertinentia,* ed. N. L. Tunickij (Tunitsky) (London, Variorum Reprints, 1972); English translation of the Life of St. Clement in *Kiril and Methodius,* loc. cit., 93–126.
    10. VIII Homilia, PG 63, col. 501.
    11. Michael Choniates (Acominatus), *Works,* ed. S. Lambros, 2 (Athens, 1880): 296.
    12. VC, ch. 14.
    13. VC, ch. 16.
    14. E.g., a tenth-century panegyric to Cyril and Methodius, in P. A. Lavrov, *Materialy po istorii vozniknoveniya drevneishei slavyanskoy pis'mennosti* (Leningrad, 1930), p. 83; the Life of St. Clement by Theophylact of Ohrid in *Monumenta ad SS Cyrilli et Methodii successorum vitas pertinentia,* p. 82; the *Vita* of the Princes Boris and Gleb by Nestor, an eleventh-century Russian hagiographer: ed. D. I. Abramovich, *Zhitiya svyatykh muchenikov Borisa i Gleba i sluzhba im* (Petrograd, 1916); the Life of St. Stephen of Perm' by Epiphaniy the Wise (fourteenth century: *Zhitie sv. Stefana, episkopa Permskogo,* ed. V. Druzhinin (reprint, The Hague, 1959).
    15. VM, ch. 8.
    16. See Jakobson's study and translation of the *Prologue* in his *Selected Writings,* 6, part 1 (Berlin–New York–Amsterdam, 1985): 191–206.

The Image of Greece in Modern English Literature
Asa Briggs

The literature with which I shall be directly concerned in this essay is called *modern* English literature in my title, yet James Thomson's poem "Liberty," from which I shall quote later, was written a generation before the American Declaration of Independence. For many of the British philhellenes who supported the Greeks during the War of Independence, which began in 1821, the Greek cause had been anticipated by the American cause. Indeed, it was an American philhellene, Samuel Gridley Howe, who in retrospect memorably described those philhellenes who went out to Greece to fight as "an assemblage of romantic adventurers, reckless crackbrained young men from the four corners of the world." Howe was to marry Julia Ward Howe, author of "The Battle Hymn of the Republic."

The Greek nationalist leader, Prince Alexandros Mavrokodatos, who was to preside over the first Greek national assembly in Epidaurus in January 1822, had the American constitution in mind when the first Greek constitution was promulgated — with far less confidence in its future than the framers of the American constitution had felt. He had told Colonel (later Earl) Stanhope, who during the early stages of the War of Greek Independence was a dedicated representative in Greece of the Greek committee of sympathizers in London — founded in the famous Anchor Tavern in the Strand in March 1823 — that he was an admirer of the government of the United States. Stanhope himself, a utilitarian, urged the Greeks to "Americanize" their government.

Greece in Modern English Literature

This advice was given at a time when Greece, in Stanhope's phrase, was "big with events," and Stanhope, who preferred not to be called a philhellene, wrote modestly but proudly that in the "noble work" of fighting for independence the Greeks had associated him with Lord Byron, "an alliance that at once sheds honor on me and dooms me to insignificance. My sole merit is in having felt and acted like a Greek."

Stanhope described Byron immediately after his death as England's "brightest genius" and Greece's "noblest friend," and Lady Caroline Lamb called him "mad, bad, and dangerous to know." With Byron literature and politics meet, overlap, and indeed, at times, become one. Yet when Byron had first gone to Greece in 1809 with John Cam Hobhouse, the strong sense of what Greece was like as a place preceded his sense of political involvement. In his poem "The Siege of Corinth," he writes simply:

> We forded the river and clamb the high hills,
> Never our steeds for a day stood still,
> Whether we lay in the cave or the shed,
> Our sleep full soft on the hardest bed,
> Whether we couched in our rough capote
> Or the rougher plank of our gliding boat,
> Or stretched on the beach or our saddles spread
> As a pillow beneath the resting head,
> Fresh we woke upon the morrow:
> All our thoughts and words had scope,
> We had health, and we had hope,
> Toil and turmoil but no sorrow.

The sixth Lord Byron was then twenty-two years old, and politics already burst through him as he ended his poem with the two striking lines:

> Despite of every yoke she bears
> That land is glory's still and their's.

In his better known long poem "Childe Harold's Pilgrimage," the manuscript of the opening cantos of which he took back to Britain in 1811 after his first visit to Greece, Byron invoked the "Spirit of Freedom" and apostrophized Greece in words that soon became very well known.

> Fair Greece! sad relic of departed worth!
> Immortal, though no more; though fallen, great!
> Who now shall lead thy scatter'd children forth,
> And long accustomed bondage uncreate?

Byron also translated "Sons of the Greeks Arise," the hymn of the Greek patriot and martyr, Rigas Velestinlis, who was strangled in Belgrade in 1793. Rigas himself had translated the French *Declaration of the Rights of Men* into Greek.

Byron's return, at first a reluctant return, to Greece in 1821 —not from Britain this time but from Italy where he had lived in exile since 1816—unfolded a new Greek experience. "Greece was the only place I was ever contented in," he said, and he went there on this occasion quite deliberately to help "uncreate that bondage," to act, rather than to enjoy or to observe. He did not find, however, the soldier's grave for which he hoped. There is sorrow, the missing element in 1810, in the last lines he wrote at marshy Missalonghi in 1821:

> Seek out—less often sought than found—
> A soldier's grave, for thee the best,
> Then look around, and choose thy ground
> And take the rest.

By then, of course, Byron knew Greece intimately at firsthand. Compare his picture of the country with that of James Thomson:

> Hail, nature's utmost boast! unrivalled Greece!
> My fairest reign! where every power benign
> Conspired to blow the flower of human kind,
> And lavished all that genius can inspire.
> Clear sunny climates, by the breeze main,
> Ionian or Aegean, tempered kind:
> Light, airy soils: a country rich and gay,
> Broke into hills with balmy odours crowned,
> And, bright with purple harvest, joyous vales.

There is love of Greece in these lines, but it is love based on distant contemplation, not on intimate experience. And even for Englishmen who lived in Greece and knew it well there could be something remote about their writing. Byron admired Walter Rodwell Wright, who was Consul-General for the Ionian

Islands between 1800 and 1804, when they were occupied by the British in the struggle against Napoleon. Before he went to Greece Byron wrote of Wright:

> Wright! 'twas thy happy lot at once to view
> Those shores of glory, and to sing them too;
> And sure no common Muse inspired thy pen
> To hail the land of Gods and Godlike men.

Nonetheless, Wright was not far removed in style and feeling from Thomson when he wrote of Corfu:

> Here gushing founts and springs that never fail
> Pour health and plenty through the smiling vale:
> Fair smiles the vale, the myrtle edges crown's
> And aromatic fragrance breathes around . . .
> 'twas here sequester'd midst embowring shades,
> That bright Nausicea sported with her maids,
> What time Laertes' god-like son address'd
> His tale of sorrow to her pitying breast.

Nausicea and Laertes represented ancient Greece, and it was through ancient Greece and its writers that eighteenth-century visitors approached Ottoman-controlled Greece, saluting it as the philhellenes did, or shying away from it as a sad descent from antiquity. There was often a suggestion that in time it would be liberated, but little consideration was given to how or when. Nor did all lovers of ancient Greece believe that modern Greece deserved to be free. Indeed, some antiquarians did not believe that modern Greeks could be trusted with their own ancient treasures.

They were not unchallenged, however. Byron, who knew his Greek literature, ancient as well as modern, was caustic in dismissing what he called "antiquarian twaddle": as early as 1809 he was mocking scholarly or aristocratic enthusiasts for "Phidian Greeks, misshapen monuments and maimed antiques." He was not thinking only of his fellow-countrymen and their "mutilated tours." The Germans, it has been said, particularly Winckelman who did so much to direct scholarly attention to Greek art, preferred to contemplate Greece at a distance "removed from everyday reality," which got in the way of the ideal. Byron, who was interested in bodies as in minds, would have said the opposite.

There had, in fact, been many eighteenth-century British travelers to Greece, some of them more interested in images than in words and in buildings more than in books. Some of them have been discussed recently, along with other travelers, in David Constantine's *Early Greek Travellers and the Hellenic Ideal,* an interesting study which builds on the fascinating work of Terence Spencer's *Fair Greece, Sad Relic* of 1954.

Two of the most interesting British travelers were James Stuart and Nicholas Revett, who visited Athens in 1751, the year they were elected members of the Society of Dilettanti, and stayed in Greece for two years. At Hagley Park in England Stuart was to design in 1758 a Doric temple, which has been described as the "first building of the Greek revival in all Europe," a revival which of course strongly influenced the United States and is indeed better represented here than in England. Yet Stuart and Revett did not leave literature out of their own picture. "There is perhaps no part of Europe," they declared in the first volume of their *Antiquity of Athens* (1762), "which more deservedly . . . excites the curiosity of the Lovers of polite Literature than . . . Attica and Athens, its capital city."

The pages of the "polite literature" they and their successors produced were often illustrated, nonetheless, with pictures of Greece as it was rather than as it had been and of modern rather than ancient Greeks. Such travelers felt all the passion of explorers and were willing, even eager, to shake off polite conventions when they arrived on Greek soil. Frederick North, son of the Prime Minister Lord North, who (in popular legend, at least) lost America, was one of them. He was converted to the Greek Orthodox Church. Another, Thomas Gordon, was the first Englishman to join the insurgent Greeks in 1821. In this company one highly unconventional traveler, Lady Hester Stanhope, was unimpressed by the young Byron whom she thought had very little out of the ordinary to say and was not as good-looking as he was made out to be.

Travel books must figure prominently in any account of the impact of one country on another or on its literary and artistic styles. It is interesting to compare J. B. S. Morrit's *Account of a Journey Through the Morea* (1750)—Morrit was "Arch-Master" of the Dilettanti Society and a founder of the Travellers' Club—with W. H. Leake's *Travels in the Morea* (1830), which he followed with *Travels in Northern Greece* (1835) and *Peloponnesica* (1846). According to Douglas Dakin's pioneering study of British and American philhellenes, published in 1955, "Nearly all the travellers who went to Greece in the thirty or forty years before the Greek Revolution—and their numbers increased when Western Europe was cut off from the British during the Napoleonic Wars—were agreed that even the Greeks of 'the lower orders'—that was the usual phrase at the time for the masses of the population—were conscious of their glorious past and of their existing degradation." And while some of the travelers ridiculed the current forms of Greek language and religion, the very fact of their close encounter with Greece was significant both in the history of literature and in politics. They provided the kind of influence on opinion which could not have been provided by traders and financiers, although it is important to note that interest in Greece for economic reasons also increased in the economically advanced Britain of the late eighteenth and early nineteenth centuries. Traders and financiers were less concerned with ideals, of course, than they were with profits. By contrast, the Germans approached Greece through their concern for humanistic ideals.

At this point I must turn to generalization. There are two kinds of country—countries on the map and countries in the mind. Writers and artists fuse, or confuse, the two. So do we all even when we travel. For the large majority of people who do not travel outside their own countries, all other countries are, of course, countries in the mind. Yet such a lack of direct experience never precludes love—or hate—at a distance.

For British writers and artists, at least from the seventeenth century onward, Greece, whether they had visited it or not, was never just one other country. It belonged to a bigger mental map. Thus, when John Keats, most romantic of romantic poets, author of the wonderful "Ode on a Grecian Urn," read Chapman's translation of Homer—a sturdy Tudor version, very different from the published verse of Alexander Pope in the early eighteenth century—he felt that he was traveling in "realms of gold." And the traveller, with Homer in front of him in Chapman's translation, was peopling the realms of gold also, bringing the ancient Greeks back to life, it seemed. He could travel to Greece, therefore, as in space travel, with as much of the past in the experience as there was of the prersent. For another poet, Leigh Hunt, Chapman blew "as rough a blast as Achilles could have desired to hear."

Past, therefore, was directly related to present and, later in the nineteenth century, philosophy and history seemed to share the same relevance as poetry. "Aristotle and Plato, and Thucydides," wrote the great headmaster of Rugby, Thomas Arnold, usually thought of as the founder of the British public school system, "are most untruly called ancient writers: they are virtually our own countrymen and contemporaries."

Hellenism, fascination with ancient Greece, survived as well as preceded philhellenism, romantic love of modern Greece. "That man is little to be envied," Samuel Johnson had explained, "whose patriotism would not gain force upon the plain of Marathon." He made the remark during a visit, not to a Greek island but to the island of Iona off the coast of Scotland, yet the location did not detract from the forcefulness of his assertion. And it was a very different Englishman of a very different generation, the essayist/philosopher/political economist/social theorist, John Stuart Mill, who claimed boldly that "the battle of Marathon even as an event in English history is more important than the battle of Hastings," the decisive battle won by William the Conqueror against the Saxons in 1066 following the last great invasion of England. No Englishman could have said more.

Ancient Greece obviously provided a powerful stimulus not only to the imagination but to declarations of faith in universal human values. And significantly it was at Marathon that

Byron dreamed in his poem "Don Juan" that modern Greece might be free. "Who would be free themselves must strike the blow," he had already written in "Childe Harold," and he never lost that conviction. He always preferred the Greece that he knew at firsthand to the Greece of the books, and he never tried to people Greece with ancient Greeks dressed in modern clothes, Greek or British. Greeks, he knew, could be lovable, but they could also be rascals. Stanhope, "the typographical Colonel," as Byron called him (because he wanted the insurgent Greeks to be equipped not only with arms but with a printing press) knew this too. While he did not hesitate to flatter the modern Athenians as "worthy descendents of ancient, learned, valiant and famed people," Stanhope noted also how absurdly disappointed some British travelers were when they met modern Greeks who did not conform to classical expectations. They came "expecting to find the Peloponnese filled with Plutarch's men," he wrote, "and returned thinking the inhabitants of Newgate more moral." (Newgate was London's notorious prison.)

For Byron in particular, however, while Greeks could at times "disgust" him, Greece was preferable to "hapless England" which in the early nineteenth century, in his view, had some of the characteristics of a jail. In his own words, he was "born for opposition," and when he delivered his first speech in the House of Lords in 1812 it was in opposition to a government bill seeking to deal with Britain's Luddites (machine breakers) by making machine breaking a capital offense. "I have been in some of the most oppressed provinces of Turkey," he told the Lords, "but never under the most despotic of governments did I behold such squalid wretchedness as I have seen since my return in the very heart of a Christian country." Byron admired Napoleon, and was to write of the death of King George III in his poem "The Vision of Judgment" in 1820

> In the first year of freedom's second dawn
> Died George the Third, although no tyrant, one
> Who shielded tyrants, till each sense withdrawn
> Left him no mental nor external sun;

> A better farmer ne'er brushed dew from lawn,
> A worse king never left a realm undone.

"The first year of freedom's second dawn," 1820, one year before the struggle for Greek independence began, saw the upsurge of the revolutionary movement in Italy, with which Byron also was associated: this was the prelude to Greek independence, although an unsuccessful prelude. The "first dawn," of course had been the French Revolution of 1789. It was the fact that for Byron the English were not free that lent vigor to his effort to support the Italians and Greeks in their fight for freedom. His political as well as his poetic reputation outside England was greater than his reputation inside it, and it was to last longer outside. Nonetheless, Hippolyte Taine, the French critic, was to write of Byron in his four-volume *History of English Literature,* published in 1863–1864, that he was so great and so English that "from him alone we shall learn more truths of his country and of his age than from all the rest together." While Byron was alive, Stanhope had shrewdly noted that although he professed "deep antipathy to the English," he was "always surrounded by Englishmen and in reality preferred them (as he did Italian women) to all others."

For all Byron's sympathies with the French—indeed, because of them—he was critical, as were many of his British contemporaries, of Russian ambitions, as he saw them, in Greece. He had written in "The Age of Bronze":

> Better still toil for masters, than await
> The slaves of slaves before a Russian gale

There was little sympathy in nineteenth-century Britain before or after Greek independence for the view from Moscow or from St. Petersburg. Frederick Douglas's *Essay on Certain Points of Resemblance between the Ancient and Modern Greeks,* published in 1813, sets the scene in this respect. So also did the Greek insurrection of 1770, which has been aptly described as "only one brief passage in the interminable rivalry and warfare of Russia and Turkey." Although tsarist Russia was drawn directly into the struggle for Greek independence, it worked through the Orthodox Church and through traditional elites in Greece who wished, as a twentieth-century historian, Richard Clogg, has put it, to substitute their own oligarchical rule for that of the Turks.

Byron and the British philhellenes, even when they were not democrats, disliked oligarchy, and when they looked to the future they believed that Greek nationalism carried with it a universal message that would spread. Byron's fellow poet Shelley, beside whom he lived in Italy before he returned to Greece in 1823, wrote of a "renewal of liberty" from which Englishmen as well as Greeks would benefit. "This is the age of the war of the oppressed against the oppressors," he exclaimed. Poets were "unacknowledged legislators of the world" and had the duty to summon the oppressed to shake off their chains. Byron's attitude to poetry was very different, but his attitude to oppression was not.

Shelley never went to Greece, nor did many of the other British philhellenes. He met a few Greeks in Italy, but his Greece was beyond doubt a country of the mind, as his poems reveal. "We are all Greeks," he could write; Keats, who died in 1821 just before the outbreak of the Greek revolt, shared the sentiment. Byron was a friend of Shelley, but a condescending and often vicious critic of Keats; "a Cockney Mannickin," he called him, "a tadpole of the Lakes." It was an unfair judgment. Indifferent to the visual arts of Greece—and in this respect far less imaginative than Keats—Byron tended to be contemptuous of anyone who wrote about Greece, even ancient Greece, without actually visiting it. "It is one thing to read the *Illiad* with Mount Ida above," he wrote, "and another to trim your taper over it in a smug library."

Byron's descriptions of Greece, the first of them based on what Peter Quennell, his biographer, has called "random travels," remain as interesting as his invocations to Greek freedom; they sound true to modern travelers to Greece.

> The isle is now all desolate and bare
> Its dwellings down, its tenants passed away.

or

> High barrows without marble or a name
> A vast untilled and mountain-skirted plain.

or
> Troops of untended horses, here and there,
> Some little hamlets with new names uncouth.

Byron was always wary of claiming too much. Thus he called his long poem "Don Juan"—which has been hailed by some critics of English literature as "our great English epic"—"a lowly lay of mine." He dared not invoke the ancient muse from her "sacred hill," he explained, even though she had

> Wandered by thy vaunted rill;
> Yes sighed o'er Delphi's long deserted shrine,
> Where, save that feeble fountain, all is still.

In a later canto he added that he could never dream of comparing himself with immortal Homer.

> To vie with thee would be about as vain
> As for a brook to cope with ocean's flood.

"Don Juan" has won more praise from later generations than "Childe Harold," Byron's descriptive and contemplative poem which he published soon after his first return from Greece, although "Don Juan" has usually been appreciated more outside Britain than inside it. It must be read within a European, not a British, context. Yet while T. S. Eliot, writing in 1937, acknowledged that "Don Juan" was a remarkable work, he described Byron as a "Scottish poet," a description Byron would have abhorred, to be compared with Sir Walter Scott, whom Byron respected, and with Robert Burns. In judging Byron's poetry he left out the European context altogether. Byron had written too many short extempore poems, Eliot argued, to maintain any kind of quality or even consistency in his verse. This was an inadequate judgment made by a twentieth-century poet. After all, Byron produced in "Don Juan" a romantic hero, who stood out in Taine's phrase as the "ruling personage of the age," and few poets do this. Nonetheless—and there was irony here—Byron himself preferred pre-romantic verse to most of the poetry of his contemporaries; Pope for him was "the best of poets." And there was a deliberately bantering, debunking tone in his style which can irritate modern readers as much as it irritated his contemporary, Thomas Love Peacock, who could banter and debunk himself. Byron could apply this tone to himself.

> When a man hath no freedom to fight for a home
> Let him combat for that of his neighbours;
> Let him think of the glories of Greece and of Rome
> And get knocked on the head for his labours.

We are reminded of two other of Byron's lines:

> Society is now one polish'd horde,
> Formed of two mighty tribes, the *Bores* and *Bored*.

Who else among major British poets would have had the effrontery to rhyme "intellectual" with "hen-peck'd-you-all"?

The Victorians, unlike Taine, preferred Keats and Wordsworth—and Byron had no respect for the latter either—to Byron himself. By then, however, it was not only Byron's poetry which looked out-of-date, but his whole style of life. Byron believed in the goddess Fortune; the mid-Victorians believed in self-help and hard work. Many of them were as critical of aristocratic virtues as they were of the kind of aristocratic vices that Byron seemed to present in flamboyant abundance. Sir Robert Peel, the son of a cotton spinner, who was at Harrow School with Byron, was a new hero of the age, and as Walter Bagehot pointed out in a brilliant essay of 1856, Peel and Byron were in complete contrast with each other. By "a blow of the imagination" Byron "elicited a single bright spark of light on every subject." His opinions erupted; his mental action was "volcanic." By contrast, Peel's opinions "resembled the daily accumulating . . . deposits of a rich alluvial soil." Peel was a statesman for forty years; Byron "would not have been a statesman for forty days."

Bagehot was a keen enough historian, however, not to miss the political significance of Byron's Greek connection. It was, after all, the London *Times* which wrote on Byron's death that "the noblest of enterprises," the delivery of Greece, which "employed the whole of Lord Byron's latter days . . . was a cause worthy of a poet and a hero."

Many travelers to Greece later in the nineteenth century obviously thought of Byron on their travels as well as of Homer, although travel was intermittent during the 1830s, 1840s, and 1850s, when Greek independence proved less exciting in practice than the struggle to achieve it. The record of the struggle was set out at length by the historian George Finlay who, when Byron first met him in Greece in 1823, was taken for Shelley's ghost. Finlay himself took an active part in Greek liberation through all its phases. "To me," Finlay wrote, "Greece is a second country, the scene of my boyish enthusiasm and the hope of my maturer years." When Finlay died in 1875, once again the *Times* found the right words to praise Greek liberation. "It would take Shakespeare's richness of language to give adequate expression to the intensity of passion with which the modern Greeks rose to destroy the power of their masters." Finlay is a neglected historian, but a professor at Harvard told him that he "would rather be author of your *Histories* than prime minister of England."

Finlay dealt mainly in facts. Another writer on Greece (and Byron) the Cornishman Edward Trelawny, buccaneering friend of Shelley and Byron, dealt mainly in myths. Byron said that Trelawny "would not tell the truth to save his life." Yet his life was both more dramatic—difficult though that was—and more prolonged than Byron's. Trelawny did not die until 1881, six years after Finlay, but he might well have been killed nearly sixty years earlier when he was attached after Byron's death to Odysseus, Greek rebel leader fighting from a mountain stronghold. Trelawny married Odysseus's thirteen-year-old sister and loved to wear Greek peasant clothes. He sat as a model for Millais and figures as the old seaman in Millais's painting "North West Passage." He was described by a young rebel poet of a new Victorian generation, Algernon Swinburne, as "world-wide liberty's lifelong lover."

Trelawny's *Records of Shelley, Byron and the Author,* published in 1858, is not all myth, however. Compare his realistic account of Arcadia with the pre-Victorian, Victorian, and post-Victorian myth of Arcadia (ending in musical comedy) as a land of nymphs and shepherds.

Our road was a mere mule path for about two leagues, winding along the bed of a brook, flanked by rugged precipices. In this gorge, and a more rugged path about it, a large Ottoman force, principally cavalry, had been stopped in the previous autumn, by barricades of rocks and trees, and slaughtered like droves of cattle by the wild and exasperated Greeks.

Or compare Trelawny's account of Mount Parnassus, where he lived alongside Odysseus, with the myths of ancient Parnassus which stirred Victorian schoolboys as keenly as they stirred Victorian poets like Tennyson and Swinburne. A cavern became Odysseus's and Trelawny's citadel. "We built boarded houses within it, and stored it with all the necessaries and many of the luxuries of life besides immense supplies of arms and munitions."

Mid-Victorian attitudes toward nineteenth-century Greece during the fight for independence, and the often painful and seldom romantic process of nation-building which followed it, do not figure prominently in two excellent recent books on the Victorians and ancient Greece by Richard Jenkyns and Frank Turner, the first published in Britain and the second in the United States. Nor do either of them mention the publication of Murray's *Handbook for Travellers in the Ionian Islands, Greece, Turkey, Asia Minor and Constantinople,* a landmark in the routinization of Greek travel (pointing to the travel brochures of the nineteenth century) or Baedecker, who with fitting realism noted the absence of hotels in Greece.

These two recent books take the place of older and more superficial studies, like Sir Ernest Barker's essay on "Greek Influences in English Life and Thought," reprinted in his *Traditions of Civility.* Yet Barker, who was steeped in Greek thought, found the perfectly apposite nineteenth-century quotation from the great Victorian lawyer, Sir Henry Maine: "Except for the blind forces of nature, nothing moves in this world which is not Greek in origin."

Maine conveniently left out not only steam engines but Hebraic influences in the nineteenth-century world, although the relationships between Greek and Hebrew, pagan and Christian, were favorite themes for many Victorian writers, not least Matthew Arnold, son of Arnold of Rugby. As Jenkyns has put it in summary form, "Ancient Greece preoccupied some of the finest minds of the last century, and thus, directly and indirectly it became a pervasive influence, reaching even to the edges of popular culture." "My uncle's thoughts," wrote the nephew of the great British Whig historian, Thomas Babington Macaulay, were often "weeks together" in Latium and in Attica rather than in Middlesex.

Jenkyns has noted also the "extraordinarily wide" range of nineteenth-century British books which could not be printed without the use of Greek type. It included not only serious nonfiction like Ruskin's *Modern Painters,* Newman's *Apologia,* John Stuart Mill's *Essay on Liberty,* and Matthew Arnold's *Culture and Anarchy,* but also Thackeray's novel *Pendennis,* all but one of George Eliot's novels, Thomas Hardy's *Jude the Obscure* (in his first novel *Desperate Remedies* there were *two* characters called Cytherea), *Lorna Doone, Tom Brown's Schooldays, Eric or Little by Little,* and two of Gilbert and Sullivan's operettas. And though less Greek type is used, and there is less knowledge of the ancient Greek language in twentieth-century Britain than there was in the nineteenth century, the appeal persists for readers—and travelers. "There is a special kind of presence here in this land, in this light," wrote the widely read author Lawrence Durrell in his book *The Greek Islands* in 1978. "It is not uncommon for visitors of sensibility to have the almost uncomfortable feeling that the ancient world is still there just out of sight."

It was sometimes within sight, it seemed to the Edwardian poet, James Elroy Flecker. Addressing a poet a thousand years hence in one of his lyrics, Flecker placed himself deliberately in the position of a Greek poet thousands of years before when he wrote.

> But have you wine and music still
> And status and a bright eyed love?

This was communicating across the centuries in a nostalgic rather than an intellectual way.

I cannot leave out a greater poet who changed the image of Greece and did not copy his predecessors. W. B. Yeats looked back at Greece not in terms of Hellenic Greece, but of Byzantium, largely ignored by the Victorians.

> The unpurged images of day recede;
> The Emperor's drunken soldiery are abed;
> Night resonance recedes, night-walkers' song
> After great cathedral gong;
> A starlit or a moonlit dome disdains
> All that man is,
> All mere complexities,
> The fury and the mire of human veins.

It is significant, perhaps, that it is Byzantium, too, which has inspired the work of one of Britain's great twentieth-century historians, Sir Steven Runciman. A whole history has been recast. "Sailing to Byzantium," the title of one of Yeats's poems, has become as exciting an exploration as "sailing to Troy," although James Joyce's *Ulysses* returns further back in time to the oldest of odysseys.

There are so many layers of experience in Greece that old as well as young turn again and again to it. To Byron it was the "land of friendship and adventure," and when he first returned from Greece in 1811 at the age of twenty-three "the precious gift" of youth already "seemed to be slipping away from him like a prodigal's fortune." No man, he believed, ought to live after thirty when enjoyment ceases. Whole generations of writers and travelers have proved him wrong. In the light of the wisdom of age many lovers of Greece have turned again to Greek wisdom. Yet it is easy to understand why for the Greeks themselves there may be too many layers of experience. In conclusion, two quotes, not from an English poet but from a twentieth-century Greek poet, George Seferis, seem particularly appropriate. In both Seferis is aware of the burdens.

> Because we have known so well this tale of man
> Wandering among broken stones, three or six thousand years,

> Digging in ruined buildings which could perhaps have been
>   our homes
> Trying to remember dates and deeds of heroes.

That is general, the second is specific:

> I woke with this marble head in my hands:
> It exhausts my elbows, and I don't know where to put it down.

This haunting image lingers as long as the images of "Ode on a Grecian Urn." There is more than one Greece on the map and in the mind, but it is Greeks themselves who must decide what it has been and what it shall be.

Tsarist Russia and Greek Independence
Barbara Jelavich

In most accounts of foreign involvement in the Greek revolution of the 1820s the emphasis is placed on the activities of Britain and France and on the influence of the western philhellenes on their governments. Although indeed in the final stages of the establishment of an independent Greece, British and French statesmen did play the leading roles, Russia was associated in these actions and its victory over the Ottoman Empire in 1829 made the final settlement easier to achieve. In addition, and what is often overlooked, in the first year and a half after the outbreak of the revolution, the tsarist government alone among the great powers attempted to organize an international intervention, and it almost went to war over issues connected with the Greek revolt. This essay deals with this period of Russian diplomacy and with the favorable reception which the revolution received in both liberal and conservative circles.[1]

Certainly, of the states involved in eastern affairs, Russia had the closest relationship with the Greeks of the Levant. The strongest link was, of course, the common Orthodox faith, which Russia alone among the great powers shared with the Greek nation. The patriarchate of Constantinople, the supreme Orthodox institution, was regularly controlled by Greeks, who through the operation of the Ottoman millet system had won the prime position among the Christian Orthodox population of the empire. Russian ties with Ottoman Greek society thus gave St. Petersburg a better position in regard to all of the Balkan Christians.

Russians and Greeks were also brought together by other than religious affiliation. During the eighteenth century, with common land and sea borders, Russia and the Ottoman Empire were drawn into an ever closer relationship. In dealing with the Porte, a term used to refer to the Ottoman government, the Russian diplomats were regularly in touch with Greeks in their functions as officials or interpreters. Enjoying the leading political position among the non-Muslim citizens of the empire, Greeks were given high positions, the most important of which were the governorships (hospodarships) of the two Danubian principalities, Wallachia and Moldavia. They similarly held posts as secretaries and interpreters (dragomen) for Ottoman officials, and they thus became the intermediaries in negotiations concerning political and economic affairs with Western as well as with Russian diplomats.

Common economic interests also joined Russians and Greeks. At the beginning of the nineteenth century Greek merchants dominated the commercial life of the empire; their ships carried Russian grain and had the right to fly the Russian flag. As Greek commerce continued to prosper, colonies of merchants were established throughout Europe; in Russia Odessa became a center of Greek activity. Because of their prominence in Eastern trade and in the life of the empire, the Russian government appointed Greeks as its consuls throughout the Balkans, but particularly in Greek-inhabited lands.

Such religious, political, and economic ties led often to close personal relations. Phanariot families contributed members to the Russian army and bureaucracy; many married into the Russian aristocracy. It should, however, be noted that despite this situation Russians were primarily in touch with those Greeks who were prominent in Ottoman affairs, either as church officials, members of the bureaucracy, or merchants and bankers, all of whom had their center in Constantinople. Russian officials had less knowledge of and fewer links with the Greeks of the Peloponnesus or the mainland.

As a great power embarked upon a period of imperial expansion, Russia had in the eighteenth century shown a great interest in Greek-inhabited lands. Multiple plans were elaborated for the partition of the Balkan peninsula, the most famous of which was Catherine the Great's Greek project, which envisioned the creation of a state under the rule of her grandson Constantine, with its capital at Constantinople. In the course of a war with the Ottoman Empire between 1768 and 1774 a Russian fleet operated in Greek waters, and Russian agents initiated a disastrous revolt in the Peloponnesus. During the Napoleonic Wars Russia occupied the Ionian Islands from 1800 to 1807. Thus before 1821 the Russian government had concerned itself with Greek political problems, and it had supported rebellion and a breakup of the Ottoman Empire when these actions served state interests.

Although previous wars between Russia and the Ottoman Empire had failed to advance the cause of Greek freedom, they did result in the conclusion of a series of treaties which both benefited some Greeks and allowed Russia increased rights of intervention in Ottoman affairs. The most important, the Treaty of Kuchuk Kainardji of 1774, was to be the most controversial. It gave the Russian government the right to concern itself with the affairs of the Danubian principalities and the islands of the Archipelago as well as some ill-defined rights in regard to the Ottoman Orthodox population in general. Article VII contained a statement that the Ottoman government would "protect constantly the Christian religion and its churches." The treaty also assured Russia of basic commercial rights. In the next years other agreements were signed which reaffirmed or extended the Russian privileges. By 1821 the Russian government had thus gained a special position, based on treaties, in regard to its commerce, its right of intervention in the Danubian principalities and the Greek islands, and its relationship with the Balkan Orthodox. In all three of these areas of concern Russian diplomats were most likely to deal with Greek subjects of the Ottoman Empire.

With this situation it is easy to understand why Russia became a center of Greek conspiracy and why the revolutionary leaders were able to involve so many who were in Russian service. In 1814 in Odessa three Greek merchants organized the Filiki Etairia (the Friendly Society), which was to play a major role in the first stages of the revolt. From its founding the Etairia aimed at gaining official Russian support and its hopes were high. After all, in the past Russian leaders had talked a great deal about protecting Orthodox Christians; Tsar Alexander I was believed to be sympathetic to the Greek cause. In recruiting agents and supporters, the society had no hesitation about using the Russian name freely and encouraging the illusion that the movement enjoyed imperial favor. In addition, well aware that it needed a leader of European stature, the Etairia turned to the most prominent Greek national in the Russian government.

In Russian relations with the Greek revolution, the name of Ioannis Capodistrias is of principal importance.[2] Born in the Ionian Islands in 1776, Capodistrias held office during the Russian occupation at the time of the wars with France. In 1809 he formally entered Russian service and rose rapidly in its ranks. He nevertheless maintained a constant interest in Greek affairs and in the question of national liberation. Here he favored a cautious and careful policy, convinced that education and cultural development should precede measures taken toward independence. In 1815, Alexander I, who had come to rely on his advice, offered Capodistrias the position of secretary of state for foreign affairs, a post which he shared with Karl Nesselrode. Before accepting this high office, Capodistrias warned the tsar of the difficulties inherent in his appointment and of the possibility that at some time his obligations as a Russian official might conflict with his sentiments and duties as a Greek patriot. The Greeks, and he named specifically the inhabitants of the Ionian Islands and their neighbors, might call upon him.

> Sire, these men suffer and hope. Seeing me near you, they will hope even more and will overwhelm me with their just grievances. I would requite them with ingratitude, I would neglect my duties toward my native land, if, in order to get rid of them, I would consider myself as having nothing to do with Greece [*comme étranger de la Grèce*]. But I feel myself incapable of that sacrifice. It would thus be necessary

that I maintain personal relations with them, and these relations would excite the distrust of England and the other cabinets. I cannot foresee anything good in such a situation—anything of use for the service of Your Majesty; for the Greeks, nor for myself.[3]

Although Capodistrias did accept the post, his fears about a possible conflict of interest were realized when in 1817 the Etairia requested that he become its leader. Well aware of the dangers in the situation, Capodistrias rejected the offer and evidently informed the tsar. After his second refusal in 1820, the society turned to Alexander Ipsilanti, a general in the Russian army and an aide-de-camp to the tsar. When he accepted, plans for action were accelerated. The center of the conspiracy was an estate near Kishinev where the Etairia assembled arms and men; money for the rebellion was collected throughout the southern regions. The local governors, Gen. A. F. Langeron, with his headquarters in Odessa, and Gen. I. N. Inzov in Bessarabia, were apparently aware of these activities. Exactly what Capodistrias knew or what he told the tsar is difficult to ascertain, but certainly neither Alexander I nor his minister approved of the specific plan for rebellion formulated by the Etairia and its friends at this time.

Although the goal was Greek independence, the Etairia chose the Danubian principalities as the location for its first action. These provinces were adjacent to the southern Russian lands which served as the headquarters for the organization of the revolt. The commanding position of Phanariot Greeks as governors of Wallachia and Moldavia, and the presence of Greeks in other influential positions were also significant in this decision. In addition, an agreement was made with the Romanian leader, Tudor Vladimirescu, who in January 1821 commenced an insurrection which had primarily social and economic objectives.[4] However, most important, despite the previous negative reaction, the Etairia leaders were convinced that Russia would indeed intervene once the revolt started. They expected a violent Ottoman reaction; the resultant atrocities would both stir up Russian sentiments and involve treaty stipulations. Russian armies would then be forced to march. Thus on February 22/March 6, 1821,⁵ after crossing from Bessarabia into Moldavia, Ipsilanti included in his proclamation announcing the Greek uprising, the words: "Move, o friends, and you will see a Mighty Empire defend our rights!"⁶ He also addressed an appeal to Alexander I, hoping to turn this declaration into a reality.

Despite the expectations of the Greek leaders, the revolution was the wrong rebellion, at the wrong time, and in the wrong place. The Russian government not only had an eastern program, which had resulted in the treaties previously mentioned, but it also had a far more important western policy. In 1815, after a quarter century of devastating war, the European great powers had concluded a peace, and they were united by two treaties of alliance. The first, the Quadruple Alliance of 1814, which became the Quintuple Alliance in 1818 with the addition of France, and the second, the Holy Alliance, sponsored in particular by Alexander I, obliged the European courts to consult together and to uphold the peace. In the next years the three conservative powers, Russia, Prussia, and Austria, cooperated closely to guard against the revolutionary movements which they saw as the chief menace to European peace and stability. In January 1820 a revolt broke out first in Spain and then in Portugal. In July, a similar movement forced King Ferdinand of the Kingdom of the Two Sicilies to accept a constitution. Meeting in Troppau in October the representatives of Austria, Russia, and Prussia came to an agreement on their right to intervene should a legitimate government be overthrown by revolutionary action. Assembling again at Laibach (Ljubljana) in January 1821, they approved an Austrian military action in Naples to restore Ferdinand's autocratic position; during the meeting news arrived of a revolt in Turin on February 26/ March 10.

At both Troppau and Verona, Alexander I, working closely with the Austrian chancellor, Clemens von Metternich, enthusiastically supported the actions taken to end the rebellion in the Italian peninsula. Deeply concerned about similar outbreaks throughout Europe, which could have repercussions in Russia, the tsar had come to believe that a revolutionary central committee had been organized and was actively engaged in stirring up revolts wherever possible. He thus saw a common thread linking all of the movements to one controlling center. When the news of the revolts in the Danubian principalities reached him at Laibach, his strong reaction could be predicted. After the Vladimirescu uprising Nesselrode on February 23/March 7 sent an instruction to the Russian ambassador at Constantinople, Grigorii Aleksandrovich Stroganov, expressing his disapproval and emphasizing that at Troppau and Laibach the "allies had firmly decided to oppose a common dike against the flood of revolutions which threatens once more to convulse Europe."[7] The reaction to Ipsilanti's action was bound to be even stronger; the Etairia leader's proclamation calling upon the Greeks to rise up against tyrants and to fight for liberty was not apt to appeal to a conservative ruler bent upon suppressing revolts in other areas. Alexander condemned Ipsilanti's conduct, struck his name from the army list, forbade him from ever returning to Russia, and informed him clearly that "he could not count on any aid, nor even on any mark of interest on our part, as long as he misguided his compatriots and led them to inevitable misfortunes."[8] The tsar's reaction was reflected also in a letter written by Capodistrias from Laibach to a close friend.

> The emperor has highly disapproved of those [means] which Prince Ipsilanti appears to wish to employ to deliver Greece. At a time when Europe is menaced everywhere by revolutionary explosions, how can one not recognize in that which has broken out in the two principalities the identical effect, the same subversive principles, the same intrigues which attract the calamities of war and a military occupation to one of the peninsulas and in the other—the most dreadful plague yet of demogogic despotism."

If such indeed was "the origin and character" of Ipsilanti's revolt, then, Capodistrias concluded, "all is lost for the unfortunate Greeks."[9]

The attempt to start a revolution in the principalities was soon to end in a total disaster. Although the Etairia was able to attract about 5,000 men to its side, the Greek movement soon came into conflict with that of Tudor Vladimirescu. Deprived of support from local Romanians as well as from the great powers, Ipsilanti faced certain defeat. The decisive battle was fought at Drăgăşani on June 7/19; by the end of the month the last Greek bands had been crushed and Ipsilanti had fled into the Habsburg Empire. At the commencement of the rebellion the Ottoman army had entered the principalities, where it was to remain for sixteen months.

The defeat of the Etairia did not, of course, mark an end to the revolution. By early April revolts had broken out in other Greek regions, particularly in the Peloponnesus and the islands. Although the Etairia was involved here too, it did not play as important a role in the events. Moreover, since Russia did not have a fleet in the Mediterranean and since its borders were no longer directly adjacent to the centers of rebellion, the Russian diplomats of necessity had to cooperate with other governments, in particular the French and British, in dealing with the affairs of the Greek lands themselves. Henceforth Russian attention centered primarily on events in the principalities, the threats to Black Sea commerce, and the apparent violation of certain treaty rights, in particular those in regard to the right of protection of Orthodox Christians. The center of negotiations at this time became Constantinople.

In the Ottoman capital Stroganov, despite his personal sympathy with the Greek cause, had assured the Porte of the Russian disapproval of revolutionary activity even before precise instructions arrived. Thereafter, he undertook the difficult double task of attempting to reassure Ottoman officials and at the same time urging moderation and caution in suppressing the rebellion. He understood the fears that had been aroused in Constantinople.

> Vladimirescu in his proclamations speaks of the sovereignty of the sultan and presents himself uniquely as the rectifier of the wrongs that Wallachia has suffered from the iniquitous administration of the boyars, united with the princes. Ipsilanti on the contrary, with a fatal impu-

dence that has compromised all his nation and extended a veil of mourning over Constantinople, has given the signal for a war of religion and has sworn to die or to exterminate the tyrants which have oppressed Greece for four centuries.[10]

It was also difficult for the Ottoman officials not to suspect a Russian hand in the events. They had reports on the activities of the Etairia in southern Russia and on the enthusiasm with which the news of the revolt was received there. Their suspicions were, of course, encouraged by the British ambassador, Lord Strangford, who used the opportunity to further British interests.

The revolution caught the Ottoman government at a difficult time. Its military forces were deeply engaged in attempting to suppress the rebellion of Ali Pasha of Janina. Most Ottoman officials were convinced that the Russian government was using the opportunity to back a Greek revolt. Moreover, in both the principalities and the Greek lands the rebels had massacred hundreds of Muslim civilians. In the Peloponnesus the Muslim inhabitants had been forced to take refuge in the fortified cities. This combination of Christian revolt, suspicion of Russian intrigue, and the killing of Muslims resulted in a violent reaction, whose manifestations the Ottoman government could not completely control. Throughout the empire Muslims rose against Christians and looted and destroyed church and private property. Pressure was put on the Porte to act decisively in what was rapidly becoming a religious war.

In Constantinople the anger of the government and the public turned in particular against the Phanariot Greeks who now lost their former posts in the Ottoman administration. Prominent Greeks, including the dragomen of the Porte and the fleet, were accused of treason and executed. As far as relations with Russia were concerned, the most provocative act occurred on Easter eve, April 10/22, when the 84-year-old Patriarch Grigorios was hanged at the door of his church by a band of Janissaries. Bishops, priests, and other Orthodox Christians in Constantinople died at the same time. The patriarch's body, after having been dragged through the streets and eventually dumped in the Bosphorus, was rescued and shipped to Odessa, where it was buried with high honors.

Other actions taken by the Porte similarly increased Russian-Ottoman tension. In their hunt for Greek refugees and arms, Ottoman officials began to search all ships sailing through the Straits, but they took special measures in regard to those flying the Russian flag since these could be of Greek ownership. Moreover, Greek pirate ships, which soon came to control the Aegean, were able to halt food deliveries to Constantinople. To meet their own needs Ottoman officials required ships passing through the Straits to sell any grain which they might be carrying to government stores. These and other measures affected Russian commerce, and they violated the stipulations of commercial agreements. Before the building of railroads exports from southern and, to an extent, central Russia were sent primarily through Black Sea ports and then through the Straits to their European markets. The Russian government was thus faced with the dilemma that its commerce was being severely restricted by Ottoman attempts to suppress a revolt which Russia too deplored.

However, it was not economic but religious issues that primarily affected Russian-Ottoman relations. In their negotiations with Ottoman diplomats the Russian representatives regularly accompanied their denunciation of the revolt with the advice that it be met not only with firmness, but also with justice, moderation, and administrative reform. The initial Russian policy was summarized in the tsar's instruction to Stroganov of March 31/April 12: Alexander would never encourage insurrection, but the "victims of events" should find in the Russian mission "the assistance always owed to misfortune and even more natural yet when this misfortune falls upon a nation which is united to us by the sacred ties of a common faith."[11] With this emphasis on Orthodoxy the execution of the patriarch came as a rude shock both to the religious sensibilities of the Russian leaders and to Russian prestige among the Christian people of the East. Stroganov on April 11/23 delivered a strong protest about the deaths of the patriarch and the bishops, calling particular attention to:

> "The method of their execution, the day chosen for that—a solemn and sacred day for all the rites of the Christian religion, that the Sublime Porte by Article VII of the Treaty of Kainardji *had promised to protect constantly*—these deplorable actions are scarcely proper to win back a population already desperate [*exaspérées*] and fearing a bloody reaction."[12]

Other treaties besides Kuchuk Kainardji had been violated. Although Stroganov had initially accepted the fact that the Ottoman government would have to occupy the Danubian principalities, be opposed the entrance of an army in May, an action which was carried through without adequate consultation with the Russian embassy. Throughout April, May, and June the Russian government through its ambassador in Constantinople continued to put pressure on the Porte particularly in regard to those questions where it felt that it had a legal right to intervene, such as the internal affairs of the Danubian principalities, the interruption of Black Sea commerce, and the treatment of the Greek Orthodox, who were obviously not being "protected." In his instructions to his representatives at the European courts the tsar continued to condemn the rebellion, but he also denounced the methods used in its suppression. A Russian circular dispatch of June 22/July 4 declared:

> The emperor is *fully justified* in demanding that the Turkish government *protect* the exercise of the Christian religion, the persons of its ministers, the inviolability of its temples; that it not at all carry devastation and death into the principalities of Wallachia and Moldavia, and that for the inhabitants of these countries, as for those of the islands of the Archipelago and the rest of Greece, it observe a just and constant distinction between innocence and crime."[13]

As reports of acts of violence against orthodox Greeks poured into his embassy, Stroganov personally became convinced that his government should take a stronger stand. He believed that the honor of the Russian mission was at stake and that unless Russia acted its government would appear weak or in complicity with the acts of terror being committed.[14]

The ambassador's increasingly belligerent attitude was paralleled by a modification in the views of Alexander, who left Laibach on May 12/24. About this time the tsar received word on the killing of the patriarch. Once back in St. Petersburg, away from the influence of Metternich, he began to listen more to the arguments of those who for religious, diplomatic, or humanitarian reasons called for a policy of intervention. In fact, substantial forces in Russian opinion backed this viewpoint, ranging from the military and imperialist circles which wished to continue the program of Catherine the Great, through the ardent supporters of Balkan Orthodoxy, to the liberal left, the future Decembrists, who saw in this revolution a struggle for the liberation of a people whom they identified with the Greeks of their classical educations. Thus Russian nationalists, religious circles of various views, and philhellene liberals criticized official policy.

Meanwhile, the relationship of Stroganov with the Ottoman officials became even more strained. The Porte now asked for the extradition of Greeks who had fled into Russia, a demand which received a firm refusal. In addition, the Ottoman government not only stopped commercial vessels flying the Russian flag, but also a warship carrying a postal flag, which had been sent for the ambassador's use. The crisis between the two states reached a height in July when Stroganov received an instruction, dated June 16/28, transmitting to him a strong note to the Porte, but with the authorization to modify its terms if he saw fit.[15] When delivering this message to the Ottoman government on July 6/18, Stroganov insisted forcefully on the fulfillment of its terms within its eight-day time limit. The document was written by Capodistrias and reflected his views on eastern affairs; the emphasis was on the protection of Orthodoxy rather than on the suppression of revolution.

> The cause which Russia pleads is a European cause. . . . The Sublime Porte has given Christendom the alternatives of asking whether it can remain an unmoved witness of the extermination of a Christian people, whether it can tolerate continual insults to its religion, whether it can acquiesce in the existence of a state which threatens to disturb that peace that Europe has bought at the price of so many sacrifices.[16]

The specific demands included the restoration of damaged Orthodox property; the protection of the Christian religion; an assurance that a distinction would be made between the innocent and the guilty; the reestablishment of internal tranquility and reforms to assure its maintenance; and the acceptance of Russian cooperation in organizing the internal affairs of the Danubian principalities. Should the Porte not accept these terms, the note threatened, Russia would find itself obliged to offer the Greek rebels "asylum, because they would be persecuted; protection, because they would be entitled to it; assistance, jointly with the whole of Christendom, because it [Russia] could not surrender its brothers in religion to the mercy of a blind fanaticism."

Of the specific demands, two—the just treatment of Greeks who were not in rebellion and the recognition of the Russian treaty rights in regard to the domestic affairs of the principalities—were regarded as most important. None of the terms, however, were accepted within the time limit. On July 15/27 Stroganov received an oral reply from the Ottoman officials that they had not had time to prepare an answer, but that one would arrive in three days.[17] The ambassador, an adherent of a strong stand, then broke off relations between the states and departed for Odessa as soon as the weather permitted.

The Ottoman failure to comply with the terms of the Russian ultimatum should have been followed by the Russian government's consideration of a military action—if not a declaration of war, at least an occupation of the Danubian principalities. However, despite the firm tone of the Russian note, Alexander was not prepared to adopt extreme measures without the assurance of support from the other European powers, in particular his close allies, Austria and Prussia. Although the ultimatum's phrasing had implied that the Russian government spoke in the name of Christendom, it had of course no authorization to do so. Nevertheless, efforts had been made to win support for the Russian position in regard to the Orthodox Balkan Christians and the maintenance of treaty stipulations. What Alexander now sought was the assent of the powers for Russia to assume the role in regard to the Ottoman

Empire which Austria had taken in Italy. There, acting as the agent of the alliance, Austria supplied arms to suppress revolutionary activity and aid in the restoration of the previous political order. Alexander did not, it will be noted, want a European mediation or intervention; he sought instead a mandate to deal with the Porte alone, but he wanted the backing of Christian Europe.

Even before the delivery of the ultimatum, in a dispatch of June 22/July 4, the Russian position had been stated and the support of the European courts requested.[18] The emphasis remained on the defense of Orthodoxy; revolutionary activity could not be condoned. The statement also showed Alexander's deep concern lest the European alliance be endangered.

> However, we repeat it in the name of the Emperor, Russia will never act either [on the basis of] its exclusive interests nor without cooperating with the powers with which the transactions which constitute the guarantee of general peace unite it.
>
> What it [Russia] asks, on the contrary, of these powers is that they inform it without evasion of their intentions, their wishes, and the means which they judge the most proper to assure the prosperity of the East, if the Turkish government . . . itself provokes events which it matters to it the most to avoid.

The Russian army, the document concluded, was ready to march to repel aggression or to aid in the achievement of any plan which the European governments might agree upon.

> But, today as previously . . . the Russian armies would march, not to move the frontiers of the Russian Empire forward or to give it a preponderance to which it does not aspire, but to restore peace, to strengthen the equilibrium of Europe . . . and to bring to the countries which compose European Turkey the blessing of a happy and inoffensive political life.

The Russian actions and declarations neither intimidated the Ottoman government nor won the support of the European powers. For Alexander the reaction of Austria and Britain was of principal significance, but their leaders, Metternich and the British foreign secretary Lord Castlereagh, were not impressed by the Russian arguments. They feared that, despite all the fine words about the defense of Christianity, Russian policy aimed in fact at the domination of the East, which neither could allow. Meeting in October in Hanover, they agreed upon a common policy. In the future the British government was to refuse all cooperation of the type which Alexander was requesting. Metternich, in contrast, was to appear more accommodating, but he always made his conditions for support so complicated that the tsar would hesitate to act. At the same time that the two governments were attempting to deter Russia from military action, they also pressed the Porte to grant some of the principal Russian demands. Metternich summarized them as, first, the restoration of the churches which had been destroyed; second, a guarantee of the protection of the Ottoman Christians; third, the maintenance of a distinction in the treatment of the guilty and the innocent in the Greek rebellion; and, fourth, the evacuation by the Ottoman army of the principalities and the restoration of the previous administrative system.[19] These conditions were acceptable to both Britain and Austria.

After the breaking of relations with the Porte and the failure to receive adequate support from any European government, Alexander had to decide whether he dared risk war under these conditions. Certainly, none of his demands had been met. Moreover, after the assassination of Ali Pasha in January 1822, the Ottoman army was free to turn its full strength against the Greek rebels. Reports of atrocities and massacres mounted, with the worst occurring on the island of Chios in April 1822. Within Russia influential circles continued to press for action. Among the diplomats not only Capodistrias and Stroganov[20] urged a militant attitude, but also the ambassadors, C. A. Pozzo di Borgo in Paris, K. A. Lieven in London, and I. A. Golovkin in Vienna. The generals, P. D. Kiselev, A. P. Ermolev, and I. I. Dibich, were similarly for war. Alexander, however, although he listened to varying opinions, remained attached to his European policy, and he continued to regard the Greek revolt as a manifestation of the general revolutionary spirit. In August 1821 he expressed his reservations to Capodistrias about a war with the Ottoman Empire. He feared that "the directing committee of

Paris will triumph, and no government will remain standing. It is not in my intentions to let the field free for the enemies of order."[21] In September he told the British ambassador, Sir Charles Bagot, that he agreed with Castlereagh's opinion that a war would "assist the game of the revolutionists in every country in Europe, to whom and to whom alone the late events are to be attributed."[22] This attitude was shared by others, such as the minister of finance, D. A. Gurev, and by Nesselrode, who had opposed the ultimatum and did not think that war would bring the glorious results that some expected.

Alexander's determination to maintain the European alliance and his fears about a general European revolution led him to continue through the fall and winter of 1821–22 to seek a solution through diplomacy. A military intervention was never excluded, but the tsar continued to shrink from taking such a decisive step without the assurance of at least Austrian support. In February 1822, responding to Metternich's proposals for a settlement of the crisis, he sent Nesselrode's nomination, D. P. Tatishchev, as a special envoy to Vienna.[23] At the same time the other courts were informed of the specific Russian demands, some of which went beyond those of the July ultimatum. As before, the Russian statement lacked precision, but in essence it repeated the earlier proposals: the Russian government wished to act with the Porte and agree on measures which would assure the Balkan Christians a "happy and peaceful" existence; they were to be guaranteed the free exercise of their religion, security of their persons and property, a just legal system, and a general pacification of their lands.[24]

At the same time that negotiations were proceeding in Vienna, both the Austrian and British governments attempted to persuade the Porte to meet some of the Russian demands, in particular to evacuate the the principalities. When it became apparent that this pressure was not working, Metternich did make some concessions to the Russian arguments. Although Lieven's discussions with Castlereagh were not so successful, the British government remained willing to accept the four basic Russian demands, as previously formulated by Metternich.

Unable to gain the support of the powers for a Russian war against the Ottoman Empire to be waged in the name of Europe, Alexander in May sent Tatishchev on a second mission to Vienna. In this month the Ottoman Empire commenced the evacuation of the principalities and completed the process in September. Alexander's instructions to Tatishchev reflected his preoccupation with the danger of revolution and his decision to avoid a war.

> I do not wish at all to attack the sovereignty of the Porte. All that I desire is that the system that it adopts allows Russia and its allies to cooperate with it in order to preserve the insurgent provinces from the curse of revolution. This service, as indispensable to Europe and to the Ottoman Empire itself as to our co-religionists, constitutes the true protection that Russia should exercise and assigns to it at the same time its nature and limits.[25]

Thereafter the Russian government divided its demands into two categories: first, those that dealt with general pacification and specifically Greek matters were to be solved in agreement with the European governments; second, those that concerned the principalities or Russian treaty rights would be negotiated directly between St. Petersburg and Constantinople. This decision assured the peace in 1822, but it was to cause repeated crises in Russian-Ottoman relations after the accession of Nicholas I in 1825.

Alexander's decisions in the spring of 1822 marked the collapse of Capodistrias' plans and the end of his influence on national policy. Throughout the previous months the British and Austrian governments had quite correctly singled him out as the major proponent of a military solution. Metternich consistently made him the chief culprit for the crisis. The British ambassador Bagot reported in January 1822: "The labour and intrigues of Count Capo d'Istria to bring on the war are inconceivable . . . and his enormous presumption still makes him think that he can guide the politics of Russia and lead the revolutions of Greece at the same time."[26] Certainly, of all the high Russian officials, Capodistrias was closest to Greek events and most eager that Russia intervene to stop the massacres. Conservative himself, he always placed his arguments on a basis that would appeal to the tsar, emphasizing the religious ties and the treaty stipulations which, he argued, gave Russia a right to intervene. The Greeks, according to his views, were resisting annihilation and not engaging in revolutionary activity.[27]

In addition, Capodistrias, well aware that Russia could not win the backing of the European governments, consistently favored an independent policy in eastern affairs. He opposed the appeal for a European mandate, arguing that Russia should not accept any outside mediation or interference in its relations with the Ottoman Empire. The support of other powers should be requested only to gain their assent to Russian demands, which should be formulated on the basis of independent decisions. Capodistrias also pressed for forceful measures, convinced that past experience had demonstrated that moderation and reason would not succeed in Constantinople, where these attributes were looked upon as a sign of weakness. Russian prestige, he believed, was being severely damaged by the country's reluctance to adopt a strong policy; Russian treaties were being violated, and the achievements of three wars and fifty years of diplomacy were being wiped out.

As far as concrete steps were concerned, Capodistrias in the summer of 1821 advised the occupation of the principalities. In the first months of 1822 he supported the sending of a mission to the European courts, but only with the goal of winning their approval for a Russian military action. When his choice of Stroganov as the special envoy to Vienna was rejected in favor of Tatishchev, he understood that he would henceforth have little influence on Russian policy in regard to Greek affairs. The decision in May not to go to war reduced him to despair. In a letter to Lieven of May 17/29, 1822, he expressed his bitter disappointment, and noted that future dispatches would demonstrate that

> all that we have said for a year on the great interests in the East is considered today by the imperial ministry as cancelled [*non avenu*], and that a new era is commencing with a new system. I am not able to be [a part of] either the one or the other. And the emperor agrees

> ... I love above all the good of the service and the glory of the emperor. If it is by the new system which has just been adopted that Russia is able to save its interests in the East and to assure on a solid basis the general peace and the alliance which is the guarantee of it, certainly, I would blame it on my headstrong attitude that I have not been able to understand the arrangements by which that double aim is going to be attained . . . [I have taken a] resolution to consider myself as dead for the part of the service which is conducted under a system contrary to that which we have followed until the present . . . one man more or less changes nothing as regards the nature and force of circumstances. And it is that force which will prevail. Do not doubt it.[28]

Capodistrias remained in office for a short time, but he did not involve himself in eastern affairs. In August he left for Switzerland, which was to be his headquarters until he was summoned to Greece in 1828 to be the first president of the modern nation. Before leaving Russia he had a two-hour interview with Alexander and reminded the tsar of the reservation which he had made when he accepted the position in the Foreign Ministry.

> The system that he [Alexander] has just adopted placed before me the alternative of being untrue to myself and to all the obligations that the fatherland to which I have never ceased to belong imposes upon me, or to neglect the duties of a servant of Your Majesty. Such in fact would be my situation if I still continued to believe myself capable of serving him at the Ministry of Foreign Affairs, at a time when he is going to deploy all his power against the unfortunate Greek nation.[29]

Capodistrias was certainly the most prominent member of the Russian government to support a strong policy in regard to the Greek revolution. Outside of official circles, much sympathy was also expressed for the Greek cause. As in the West, philhellene writers and poets devoted attention to it.[30] At the time of the revolt Alexander Pushkin, Russia's greatest poet, was in Kishinev.[31] Assigned to service with General Inzov because of his revolutionary writings, this twenty-one-year-old found himself in the midst of the preparations for rebellion. His initial reaction, fully reflecting the spirit of European Romanticism and philhellenism, is shown in a letter written in March to V. L. Davydov.

> The Greeks have begun to throng together in crowds under his [Ipsilanti's] three banners, of these one is tricolored, on another streams a cross wreathed with laurels, with the text *By this conquer,* on the third is depicted the Phoenix arising from the ashes. I have seen a letter by one insurgent: with ardor he describes the ceremony of consecrating Prince Ypsilanti's banners and sword, the rapture of the clergy and the laity, and beautiful moments of Hope and Freedom. . . . The rapture of men's minds has reached the highest pitch; all thoughts are directed to one theme, the independence of the ancient fatherland. . . . The first step of Alexander Ypsilanti is excellent and brilliant. He has begun luckily. And, dead, or a conqueror, from now on he belongs to history . . . An enviable lot.[32]

Greatly enthusiastic about the events unfolding near him, Pushkin joined a Masonic lodge, Ovid No. 25,[33] and hoped strongly for a Russian intervention. His letter to Davydov concluded:

> An important question: what is Russia going to do? Shall we seize Moldavia and Wallachia under the guise of peace-loving mediators? Shall we cross beyond the Danube as allies of the the Greeks and as enemies of their enemies?[34]

Two poems written in 1821 express his deep sympathy for the Greek revolt and his longing for decisive military action. The first is entitled "War" ["*Voina*"].

> It is war! At last, the banners of glory
> And honor will be hoisted to the skies,
> Whipped by tumultuous winds.
> I will behold blood, a feast of vengeance,
> As the skies rain bullets around me.
> How many impressions to be made on my thirsty soul!
> The intrepid charges of the armies,
> Quiet vigilance in camp,
> And the clash of opposing swords.
> In battle's fateful fire,
> I will be witness to the crumbling of empires,
> And the fall of warriors and their generals.
> . . . . .
> But, alas! I yet hear no call to arms.
> Troops do not march, and no one mans the guns.
> Will nothing deliver me from my monotonous musings?
> I languish, victim of a poisonous deception.

> In peacetime, I am helpless, as languor
> Lulls my soul.
> I have no will to act.
> Why do the guns remain silent?
> Why do they wait to begin?[35]

Similar sentiments are expressed in another, untitled poem.

> Loyal woman of Greece! Weep not—for he died a hero!
> An enemy bullet pierced his heart.
> Weep not! Did not you, yourself,
> Send him down the perilous and bloody road to honor?
> On the eve of battle, as if aware of his fate,
> Your husband extended to you his noble hand,
> And blessed his tearful child.
> But the summons of freedom, clear and inexorable,
> Sounded;
> And, like Aristogiton before him, he adorned his sword
> With myrtle,
> Rode fearlessly into the fight, and,
> In suffering what we must,
> Performed a great and holy deed.[36]

Although Pushkin, like many other philhellenes, soon became disenchanted with the Greek cause,[37] he nevertheless in 1829 wrote another poem in the previous romantic spirit: "Arise oh Greece" ["*Vosstan*"].

> Arise, oh Greece, arise!
> Marshall well your forces,
> The battlefield that is Olympus, Pindus, and Thermopylae
> Will share your righteous fury.
>
> Beneath lofty peaks as old as the ages,
> Youthful liberty's spark is kindled
> Amidst the marbled splendors of Athens,
> In the presence of Pericles.
>
> Land of heroes and Gods,
> You have broken the slave chains that bound you,
> Inspired by the fiery and the timeless verse
> Of Tyrtaeus, Byron and Rhigas.[38]

The opinions of the young poet, already under official surveillance because of his suspected political activities, were of course not likely to affect the attitude of the government. Russian policy was to be determined by other than romantic philhellene sentiments.

The reasons Alexander did not choose to go to war were practical as well as ideological. All wars are costly in men and money; Russian finances could ill afford dangerous conflicts. Moreover, it would have been difficult for the tsar to embark on a crusade in the interests of Orthodox Christianity without a clear agreement with the British and Austrian courts. Although Metternich made some concessions to the Russian viewpoint, the British attitude demonstrated that this power might indeed support not the Russian, but rather the Ottoman position. Finally and perhaps most important, Alexander was determined to maintain his close ties with Vienna and Berlin and to use the Russian alliance system to combat the revolutionary movements which, in his mind, were such a deadly danger to European order and stability. If the Russian army were to march, the tsar wished it to be directed against what he regarded as the greatest menace to European and Russian interests.

This policy did not, of course, signify that Russia was disinterested in Greek affairs. Diplomatic relations with the Porte were renewed in December 1824, although a new ambassador was not sent until 1827. However, no attempt was made to act independently in Greek affairs; instead in 1827 Russia joined France and Britain in a cooperative effort to obtain Greek autonomy. When Russia finally did go to war with the Ottoman Empire in 1828, the issues were concerned with the principalities, Serbia, and the previously acquired treaty rights. Although Article X of the Treaty of Adrianople did provide for Greek autonomy, this goal had already been adopted by the three powers in concert.

In conclusion, it might be well to consider how Russia regarded the question of Greek independence and what kind of a regime the tsar would have established had he won a war against the Ottoman Empire in 1822. The official communications, as we have seen, were extremely vague on Greek affairs;

they spoke only of "pacification" and the guarantee of a secure life. In January 1824, Alexander proposed the establishment of three autonomous principalities: first, eastern Greece, consisting of Thessaly, Boeotia, and Attica; second, western Greece, including Epirus, Acarnania, and the littoral with the cities of Butrino, Parga, Prevesa, and Vonitza; and, third, the Morea and Crete. It can thus perhaps be assumed that if the Russian government had won a free hand in the Greek lands either by negotiation or war, under conditions which did not compel it to allow the participation of other powers in the settlement, it would have divided the region into separate autonomous administrations similar to those in the Danubian principalities. They would no doubt have been similarly placed under Russian protection and organized with the assistance of Russian civilian and military advisers. What Russia would not have introduced, however, was the type of government the Greek revolutionary leaders were organizing in the 1820s and whose goals were expressed in the constitutions of Epidaurus (1821), Astros (1823), and Troezene (1827).[39] Such constitutional and republican administrations expressed exactly that spirit of revolution and disorder which conservative Russian tsars and statesmen deplored.

NOTES

1. The most important documentary collection for this subject is Ministerstvo inostrannykh del SSSR, *Vneshniaia politika Rossii XIX i nachala XX veka: Dokumenty Rossiiskogo ministerstva inostrannykh del* (Moscow: Izdatel'stvo Nauka, 1980), series 2, volume 4 (XII) covering March 1821 to December 1822. Cited hereafter as *VPR* 4. The collection of documents in the third volume of Anton von Prokesch-Osten, *Geschichte des Abfalls der Griechen vom Türkischen Reiche im Jahre 1821 und der Gründung des Hellenischen Königreiches* (Vienna: Carl Gerold's Sohn, 1867) should also be consulted. For a general study of the revolution, see Douglas Dakin, *The Greek Struggle for Independence, 1821– 1833* (London: B. T. Batsford Ltd., 1973). Russian policy is discussed in

1. S. Dostian, *Rossiia i Balkanskii vopros* (Moscow: Izdatel'stvo Nauka, 1972); A. V. Fadeev, *Rossiia i vostochnyi krizis 20kh godov XIX veka* (Moscow: Izdatel'stvo akademii nauk SSSR, 1958); and O. B. Shparo, *Osvobozhdenie Gretsii i Rossiia, 1821–1829* (Moscow: Izdatel'stvo mysl', 1965). For the role of other great powers, see for Austria Paul W. Schroeder, *Metternich's Diplomacy at its Zenith* (Austin: University of Texas Press, 1962); for France Edouard Driault, *Histoire diplomatique de la Grèce de 1821 à nos jours* (Paris: les Presses universitaires de France, 1925), volume 1 on the years 1821 to 1830; and for Britain Charles Webster, *The Foreign Policy of Castlereagh, 1815–1822* (London: G. Bell and Sons, Ltd., 1947).

2. For Capodistrias and the Etairia see the biography by C. M. Woodhouse, *Capodistria* (London: Oxford University Press, 1973) and his article "Kapodistrias and the *Philiki Etairia*, 1814–1821" in Richard Clogg, editor, *The Struggle for Greek Independence* (Hamden, Conn.: Archon Books, 1973), 104–34; the chapter on Capodistrias in Patricia Kennedy Grimsted, *The Foreign Ministers of Alexander I* (Berkeley: University of California Press, 1969), 226–268; and two books by G. L. Arsh, *Eteristskoe dvizhenie v Rossii* (Moscow: Izdatel'stvo nauka, 1970) and *I. Kapodistriia i grecheskoe natsional'no-osvoboditel'noe dvizhenie, 1809—1822* (Moscow: Izdatel'stvo nauka, 1976). Very important for this study is Capodistrias' memoir "Aperçu de ma carrière publique, depuis 1798 jusqu'à 1822," in *Sbornik imperatorskogo russkogo istoricheskogo obshchestva* (St. Petersburg, 1868), vol. 3, 163–292. See also Nicholas Charles Pappas, *Greeks in Russian Military Service in the Late Eighteenth and Early Nineteenth Centuries* (University Microfilms International: Ph.D. thesis, Stanford University, 1982), 429–481.

3. Capodistrias, *Aperçu de ma carrière publique*, 203.

4. For Vladimirescu's revolt, see the documents in *Revoluția din 1821 condusă de Tudor Vladimirescu: documente externe* (Bucharest: Editura academiei republicii socialiste România, 1980); the Russian reaction is discussed in Barbara Jelavich, *Russia and the Formation of the Romanian National State, 1821–1878* (Cambridge: Cambridge University Press, 1984), 16–31.

5. The double dates reflect the twelve day difference between the Julian calendar (first date given) used in Orthodox countries and the Gregorian calendar (second date) adopted by western Christianity.

6. Richard Clogg, ed., *The Movement for Greek Independence, 1770–1821* (London: Macmillan, 1973), 201. See also Prokesch–Osten, *Geschichte des Abfalls des Griechen,* vol. 3, 55–58.

7. Nesselrode to Stroganov, no. 1, Laibach, February 23/March 7, 1821, VPR 4, 36–38.

8. Nesselrode circular despatch, Laibach, March 18/30, 1821, ibid., 70–71.

9. Capodistrias to A. S. Sturdza, private letter, Laibach, March 18/30, 1821, ibid., 72–73.
10. Stroganov to Nesselrode, no. 20, April 10/22, 1821, ibid., 113–116. See also Stroganov to Nesselrode, no. 4, February 19/March 3, 1821, ibid., 23–28. For a description of these events written by a member of the Russian embassy staff in Constantinople, see Sergei Ivanovich Turgenev, "Notice sur l'insurrection des Grecs contre l'Empire Ottoman en 1821," published in Glynn R. Barratt, "A Russian View of the Greek War of Independence," *Balkan Studies*, 14 (1 1973): 47–115.
11. Alexander I to Stroganov, Laibach, March 31/April 12, 1821, *VPR*, 93–94. The tsar's attention to the humanitarian aspects of the crisis is also shown in his approval of measures to raise money in Russia to aid the victims of the revolt. See Theophilus Christopher Prousis, *Russian Cultural Response to the Greek War of Independence 1821–1830* (University Microfilms International: Ph.D. thesis, University of Minnesota, 1982), 117–159.
12. Note delivered by Stroganov to the Turkish government, April 11/23, 1821, ibid., 118–119.
13. Nesselrode circular dispatch, St. Petersburg, June 22/July 4, 1821. Prokesch-Osten, *Geschichte des Abfalls des Griechen*, vol. 3, 101–104.
14. See Stroganov to Nesselrode, no. 35, April 27/May 9, 1821, *VPR* 4, 132–133 and Stroganov to Nesselrode, no. 50, May 29/June 9, 1821, ibid., 162–165.
15. See the two dispatches to Stroganov from St. Petersburg on June 16/28, 1821. Prokesch-Osten, *Geschichte des Abfalls des Griechen*, vol. 3, 89–95.
16. Note delivered by Stroganov to the Turkish government, July 6/18, 1821, *VPR* 4, 203–207.
17. Stroganov to Nesselrode, no. 75, July 15/27, 1821, ibid., 224–226.
18. Nesselrode circular dispatch, St. Petersburg, June 22/July 4, 1821. Prokesch-Osten, *Geschichte des Abfalls des Griechen*, 101–104.
19. Webster, *The Foreign Policy of Castlereagh*, 379–380.
20. In September Alexander wrote to Nesselrode from Italy that he had just spoken with Stroganov. It was possible that once back in St. Petersburg the ambassador might advise war. Nesselrode was to make clear to him "the true interests of the European alliance" and the tsar's fixity of purpose. Alexander I to Nesselrode, September 12, 1821. A. de Nesselrode, ed., *Lettres et papiers du chancelier Comte de Nesselrode* (Paris: A. Lahure, n.d.), vol. 6, 124–125.
21. Capodistrias, *Aperçu de ma carrière publique*, 268–269.
22. Webster, *The Foreign Policy of Castlereagh*, 373.
23. See the instruction of Alexander to Tatishchev, February 5/17, 1822, *VPR* 4, 426–428.

24. Instructions to the Russian representatives in Vienna, Berlin, London, and Paris, February 6/18, 1822, ibid., 430–438.

25. Instruction of Alexander to Tatischev, May 14/26, 1822, ibid., 507–510.

26. Webster, *The Foreign Policy of Castlereagh,* 387. Bagot had reported in the previous October on Capodistrias' attitude: "He seems to me to be labouring night and day . . . to produce a state of things in which he hopes to find the rest of Europe at the opening of the Spring, if not allied with Russia in a war against the Porte, at least committed to give their sanction to Russia engaging in it singlehanded." ibid., 383.

27. Capodistrias' views are given in the material already cited and in the following documents: Capodistrias to Nikolai, private letter, June 22/July 4, 1821, *VPR* 4, 192–194; report of Capodistrias to Alexander I, July 29/August 10, 1821, ibid., 242–245; report of Capodistrias for Alexander I, August 9/21, 1821, "Second agenda sur les affaires d'Orient," ibid., 256–261; Capodistrias' report, October 11/23, 1821, ibid., 327–329; Capodistrias to Lieven, private letter, November 27/December 9, 1821, ibid., 371–376; Capodistrias' report for Alexander I, May 1/13, 1822, ibid., 500–503.

28. Capodistrias to Lieven, private letter, May 17/29, 1822, ibid., 515–516.

29. Capodistrias, *Aperçu de ma carrière publique,* 284.

30. See chapters 4 and 5 in Prousis, *Russian Cultural Response to the Greek War of Independence.*

31. See Demetrios J. Farsolas, "Alexander Pushkin: His Attitude toward the Greek Revolution, 1821–1829," *Balkan Studies,* 12 (1 1971): 57–80.

32. Pushkin to Davydov, Kishinev, March 1821. J. Thomas Shaw, ed., *The Letters of Alexander Pushkin* (Madison: University of Wisconsin Press, 1967), 79–81.

33. Henri Troyat, *Pushkin* (Garden City, N. Y.: Doubleday & Company, Inc., 1970), 179.

34. Pushkin to Davydov, Shaw, *Letters,* 81.

35. A. S. Pushkin, *Polnoe sobranie sochinenii* (Moscow: Akademiia Nauk, 1956), vol. 2, 32–33. The translation of the three Pushkin poems is by Brigit Farley.

36. Pushkin, ibid, vol. 2, 66.

37. By 1824 Pushkin's attitude toward the Greeks had changed a great deal; he wrote: "The Jesuits have talked our heads off about Themistocles and Pericles, and we have come to imagine that a nasty people, made up of bandits and shopkeepers, are their legitimate descendants and heirs of their school-fame. You will say that I have changed my opinion. If you would come to us in Odessa to look at the fellow countrymen of Miltiades, you would agree with me." Pushkin to P. A. Vyazemsky, Odessa,

June 24 or 25, 1824. Shaw, *Letters,* 161. A poem also expressed his altered views on liberal-national movements.

> Give no freedom to the flocks:
> Flocks are for slaughter and shearing,
> Their heritage, down through the ages,
> Is the club and the yoke with a rattle.

Quoted in Troyat, *Pushkin,* 180.

38. A. S. Pushkin, *Polnoe sobranie sochinenii* (Moscow: Khudozhestvennaia Lit., 1934), vol. 2, 225.

39. For the Russian conservative influence in Greek political life at the time of the revolution and later, see Barbara Jelavich, *Russia and Greece during the Regency of King Othon, 1832–1835* (Thessaloniki: Institute of Balkan Studies, 1962) and *Russia and the Greek Revolution of 1843* (Munich: Oldenbourg, 1966).

Cyprus: A Failure in Western Diplomacy
Nancy Crawshaw

A French politician recently referred to Cyprus as the graveyard of lost opportunities.[1] The island's troubled history is generally attributed to its strategic position in the eastern Mediterranean. In the age of the superpowers the existence of a large Greek Cypriot Communist party is also an important factor.

The West has an interest in seeing that Cyprus remains outside the Communist bloc. The interests of the Soviet Union are served by the continuation of the Cyprus dispute, with its damaging consequences for NATO. The Soviet Union's long-term objectives are, first, the withdrawal of the British military bases and western monitoring installations and, second, the extension of Communist influence through the local Communist party, AKEL.

There are also conflicting interests at regional and local levels. The rival claims of Greece and Turkey, motivated by a combination of mutual distrust and strategic considerations, have not been resolved by their common membership in NATO. This is an additional complication in the Cyprus conflict because of the island's proximity to the southern coast of Turkey.

On the island itself the people were divided by the traditional Greek Cypriot demand for *Enosis*—union with Greece—and Turkish Cypriot opposition to any form of government that would subject them to Greek rule, a division that goes back to the nineteenth century. Then again when Cyprus became independent in 1960 the Greek Cypriot community was itself split into the followers of the late president, Archbishop Makarios III, who accepted independence as an interim measure, and the extremists who were ready to risk even war with Turkey in the cause of Enosis.

I need review only briefly the circumstances in which the republic was set up. Cyprus achieved independence after a five-year armed struggle against British rule, in which the Turkish Cypriots sided with the British. The rebellion was organized by the Greek Cypriot underground movement, EOKA, whose objective was *Enosis*. The compromise settlement which ended the conflict was agreed to by Greece and Turkey in Zurich in February 1959, and corroborated by Britain and the Greek and Turkish Cypriot leaders. The Zurich settlement precluded Enosis and partition for all time. It enabled Britain to retain two military bases under British sovereignty, and Greece and Turkey to station small contingents of their own troops in Cyprus.

The independence of the republic, its territorial integrity, and the basic articles of its constitution were guaranteed by Britain, Greece, and Turkey. In the event of a breach of the Treaty of Guarantee, the guarantors were obliged to consult together in order to take the necessary measures to ensure that its provisions were observed. Where concerted or common action proved impossible, each of the guarantors had the right, although no legal obligation, to take individual action for the sole purpose of reestablishing the state of affairs created by the treaty. The full implementation of the treaty depended on collective action, and this is where the guarantors failed.

The constitution was intended to keep the balance of power between the Greek and Turkish Cypriot communities in the climate of distrust which followed the EOKA rising, but it gave trouble from the outset of independence. Considering the guarantors' obligations, it is surprising that they did not intervene to put the republic back on course when the constitution started to break down. Instead, a deteriorating situation was left to escalate into violence, and President Makarios proposed thirteen amendments to the constitution.

Several of the amendments struck right at the heart of Turkish interests and security, and were rejected by the Turks. Some contemporary writers saw the archbishop's action as an attempt in good faith to facilitate the smooth working of the constitution. But according to revelations published later by the Greeks, including no less an authority than General George Karayannis,[2] it was the first step in a conspiracy to overthrow the Zurich settlement by force.

The first major test for the guarantors came with the outbreak of intercommunal fighting in December 1963. They acted together in calling for a cease-fire, but the fighting continued. Greek Cypriot irregulars, backed by the police, launched a massive attack against the Turks in Nicosia, and fighting broke out in other parts of the island. Makarios, fearing intervention by Turkey, accepted Britain's offer to set up a joint peace force to restore order, but it was joint only in name, with members of the Greek and Turkish contingents making a token contribution as interpreters and liaison officers.

In accordance with the Treaty of Guarantee, Britain called an early conference of the guarantors, which was also attended by the Cypriot leaders. The Greeks demanded the termination of the Zurich treaties and called for a unitary state in which the Turks would be relegated to minority status. The Turks demanded a federal system based on the geographical separation of the two communities. The relationship between Greece and Turkey as guarantors degenerated into confrontation instead of partnership, and the seeds were sown for the political deadlock that has lasted for more than twenty years.

In Cyprus, the security situation worsened. Once fears of an immediate Turkish invasion had subsided, the Greek Cypriots looked upon the British troops as defenders of the Turkish Cypriots, and Britain's role as peace keeper became untenable. By that time the British government had warned the American government that it could no longer carry the burden alone.

British and American efforts to keep the Cyprus dispute outside the United Nations were abortive. Makarios twice rejected proposals for an enlarged peace force to include NATO and

Cyprus: A Failure in Western Diplomacy

other troops. This was not surprising, as he was committed to a policy of nonalignment and under Communist pressure to resist any extension of western influence. Moreover, he hoped to end Turkey's right of intervention, and the best chance of doing so was through the machinery of the United Nations. UN involvement now became inevitable and was in itself a setback for western diplomacy and interests.

The United Nations peace force was set up by unanimous resolution of the Security Council[3] and became operative at the end of March 1964. Initially it was sent to Cyprus for three months. The fact that it is still there more than twenty years later illustrates the intractability of the Cyprus problem rather than the weakness of the United Nations. Since the beginning, Britain has provided logistic support and the largest contingent of troops; the British contribution to the cost of the operation is second only to that of the United States. But once the UN force was established, Britain's importance as a guarantor declined and the political initiative shifted to the United States.

The Americans were faced with the almost impossible task of keeping the balance between two allies of equal importance. The first major crisis came in the summer of 1964 when Turkey, deeply concerned at the failure of the UN peace force to restore order, planned to invade the island. Faced with the prospect of war between Greece and Turkey and the possibility of Soviet intervention, President Lyndon Johnson sent a blunt warning[4] to the Turkish Prime Minister, Ismet Inonu, and the invasion plan was canceled.

After this crisis American diplomacy was intensified and the services of the former Secretary of State, Dean Acheson, were enlisted. The Acheson plan provided for union with Greece, subject to the establishment of a Turkish military base and two autonomous Turkish Cypriot cantons. The plan was a bold attempt to offer something to all the protagonists while safeguarding western defense and the strategic interests of Turkey. It was dismissed by the Greek Cypriots as disguised partition.

Before the end of the Acheson negotiations, the former EOKA leader, Colonel George Grivas, led an attack against several

Turkish Cypriot villages. His ultimate target was the Kokkina beachhead, a supply center for men and arms from Turkey. Turkey, using force for the first time, bombed the National Guard's positions and Greek villages. Kokkina was saved, but the casualties were heavy and both sides observed the Security Council's call for a cease-fire.[5]

By mid 1964 the Zurich agreements were dead for all practical purposes. The Treaty of Guarantee had proved useless. The Greek government had violated the Treaty of Alliance by sending thousands of troops to Cyprus. The Makarios administration had repeatedly violated the constitution and was therefore considered illegal by the Turkish Cypriots, who no longer recognized its authority. The government, for its part, outlawed the Turkish Cypriots as "rebels."

The drift toward partition had begun, at both geographical and administrative levels. More than 20,000 Turkish Cypriots had moved to safer areas after the Christmas 1963 fighting. When the Turkish Cypriot deputies tried to return to Parliament the following year, the government, now controlled by the Greek Cypriots, imposed conditions which would have nullified their rights under the Zurich constitution. The final blow to intercommunal co-operation came in 1966, when the Turkish judges withdrew permanently from the courts after an incident with the Greek Cypriot police.

The Kokkina battle ended, for the time being, major attacks against Turkish Cypriots. Instead, the Greek Cypriots resorted to economic pressure and blockaded the Turkish Cypriot enclaves. These tactics accelerated the trend toward partition by convincing the Turks that their safety could be assured only by the separation of the two communities. The situation remained potentially explosive. The buildup of the Greek Cypriot forces continued, with a steady influx of officers from Greece. The Turkish Cypriots fortified their enclaves under the direction of Turkish army officers. Disputes arose over the passage of police patrols. The two communities were caught up in the cycle of reprisals. The Turks took their revenge in areas where they were dominant, regardless of the dangers for their kinsmen who were at the mercy of the Greeks.

This period of relative calm ended on 15 November 1967, when the National Guard, led by Colonel Grivas, launched a major attack against the Turkish communities of Aghios Theodoros and Kophinou. Greece and Turkey were on the brink of war. At intensive peace drive was undertaken by the western powers and the UN Secretary General. But it was President Johnson's special envoy, Cyrus Vance, who finally negotiated an agreement between Greece and Turkey. The Turkish government's terms for calling off the invasion included the immediate departure of Grivas from the island, the withdrawal of all Greek and Turkish troops above the legal number, the disbandment of the National Guard, and compensation for the Kophinou victims. By January 1968 about 10,000 Greek troops had left the island, but the National Guard was not disbanded.

The Kophinou crisis forced the Greek Cypriot leaders to reverse their stand on Enosis. In January 1968 Makarios stated that a solution must now be sought within the limits of what was feasible, which did not always coincide with what was desirable.[6] His reelection as president by an overwhelming majority shortly afterwards, and the humiliating defeat of the Enosis candidate, showed that the change of direction had solid foundations in popular support.

A hopeful phase began with the start of direct talks between the two Cypriot leaders, Glavkos Clerides and Rauf Denktash. During these talks which dragged on, with interruptions, for six years, a wide measure of self-government was considered for the Turkish Cypriots within the framework of a unitary state. The crucial issue for the Turks was the extent of the control to be exercised by the central government over autonomous areas. But before this could be resolved, the National Guard under its Greek officers overthrew the Makarios government in July 1974 and installed the former EOKA gunman, Nikos Sampson, as president.

The crisis brought the Turkish Prime Minister, Bulent Ecevit, to London. The British government refused his request for joint military action and was willing to send troops only in a broadened UN operation. On 20 June Turkey landed troops in northern Cyprus. The Athens junta, which had engineered the coup, collapsed three days later, and democratic government was restored in Greece and Cyprus.

In the meantime the Security Council had called upon Britain, Greece, and Turkey to hold negotiations for the restoration of peace. On 30 July their foreign ministers signed the Geneva declaration. This contained the provision that all Greek and Greek Cypriot troops would immediately withdraw from the Turkish Cypriot enclaves and that the areas occupied by the Turkish forces would not be extended. Neither side honored these conditions.

The second Geneva conference ended in total failure. Within a few hours of its breakdown on 14 August Turkey resumed the war. When she declared a cease-fire two days later, the island was partitioned by a line running from Xeros to Famagusta. Two hundred thousand Greek Cypriots had fled to the south, where most of them became permanent refugees.

The failure of the second Geneva conference marked the demise of the Treaty of Guarantee as an instrument of collective action. The second Turkish advance precipitated an upsurge of anti–Westernism. There was little the western powers could do to defuse the situation. The Greeks withdrew from the military wing of NATO; western defense was undermined still further by an embargo on military aid to Turkey, forced upon Congress by the Greek lobby.

The Greeks argued that since Greece was a member of NATO the failure of the western powers to prevent the coup against Makarios was a serious mistake. Rumors of a coup had been circulating in Cyprus for some years, and there were several attempts to assassinate him before 1974. But when the crisis finally broke, the western powers were evidently without a contingency plan. However, but for two mistakes by Makarios himself, the coup could not have taken place. His first mistake was to bring thousands of Greek troops to Cyprus from 1964 onwards; the second was his failure to disband the National Guard after the Kophinou incident, which would have eliminated the Greek officers who later plotted against him.

Britain's failure to intervene as a guarantor in 1974 has remained a source of resentment with both Cypriot communities. Considering the hostility shown by Greek Cypriots toward the British troops in their neutral role as peace keepers both in 1963 and in 1967, it is not difficult to imagine what would have happened had they come in on the side of the Turks in 1974.

In the case of intervention on behalf of the Greeks, it was inconceivable that British troops should be used against other NATO troops, in this case Turkish. Apart from such considerations, the British government contended that it had no legal obligation to intervene unilaterally and that in each case the use of force was not feasible on military or political grounds.[7]

The 1974 war drastically changed the balance of military power. With the Turkish forces in absolute control of the north, the only weapons left to the Greek Cypriots were political and economic warfare. This they have waged relentlessly and with considerable success. Because their government is recognized, they have access to international outlets denied to the Turkish Cypriots.

At the international level a broad consensus still exists which favors direct negotiations between the Cypriot leaders under UN sponsorship. But after 1974 a new approach was necessary. With all the Turks permanently settled in the north, there was no longer any possibility of a multiregional system. This opportunity was finally lost in the talks which preceded the coup d'etat. The sole basis for a compromise now lay in territorial concessions by the Turks to allow a large number of Greek Cypriot refugees to return to their own villages under Greek Cypriot administration. In exchange, the Greek Cypriots would have to make concessions over the federal constitution.

A post-mortem on all the abortive discussions which have taken place over the past eleven years would serve no useful purpose at this stage, but certain landmarks should be mentioned.

The first breakthrough came early in 1977, when President Makarios and the Turkish Cypriot leader, Rauf Denktash, agreed to work for a "non-aligned, independent, bi-communal federal republic."[8] These guidelines, although subject to conflicting interpretations, have remained the linchpin of all subsequent discussions. The apparent ease with which Makarios and Denktash had reached agreement on general principles was deceptive. The extent of the gap between the two communities only became apparent when attempts were made to convert them into precise formulas. And the talks which were resumed shortly after the Makarios-Denktash agreement ended characteristically in deadlock.

The Greek Cypriots had nevertheless taken the first steps on the road to a federal system. Their delegate produced a map which delineated twenty percent of the island to be retained by the Turks in a federal republic. This was a tacit admission that not all the refugees would be able to return home and that Kyrenia would remain under Turkish control. Makarios had made a courageous move in the direction of reality and compromise, but his death four months later deprived the Greek Cypriots of the one leader of sufficient stature to carry the burden of unpopular concessions. Whereas Makarios had adopted a more realistic stance, his successor, President Spyros Kyprianou, put the process into reverse by clinging to certain UN resolutions as the only basis for a settlement.

It was a year before the Turkish Cypriots presented the UN Secretary-General with counterproposals. These proposals set out in detail the ingenious, if controversial, theory of "federation by evolution"[9] and are important for the light they throw on the chronic anxieties and long-term objectives of the Turks.

The Turkish constitutional outline provided for dual control at almost all levels of federal government and left the door open for the formation of a full federal republic at some distant, unspecified date. It was dismissed by the Greek Cypriot leadership as nothing more than a plan for a confederation.

The western governments intervened to break the deadlock with new proposals known as the American Plan, which was in fact drawn up by the American, Canadian, and British governments. Because of its western origins, it was automatically discredited by the Communists. After this setback all subsequent constitutional initiatives were channeled through the UN.

The Greek Cypriots came to regret their failure to consider the American Plan; many of its features were incorporated in later formulas.

The new deadlock was not broken until May 1979, when Kyprianou and Denktash signed the ten-point agreement, which reaffirmed the Makarios-Denktash guidelines. In addition, they undertook to give priority to the resettlement of Varosha and to refrain from any activity likely to jeopardize the intercommunal talks. The talks were duly resumed, but broke down after one week.

In contrast to the lack of political progress, the Greek Cypriots have made a remarkable economic recovery, despite the magnitude of the 1974 disaster. Foreign aid flowed in generously and was put to good use, but credit for this achievement must go mainly to the Greek Cypriots themselves. Within three or four years after the invasion the vast majority of refugees had some sort of housing and employment, exports were back to the preinvasion level, and hotel capacity for tourists in the south alone exceeded the preinvasion figure for the whole island.

The north presents a different picture. Economic growth and living standards lag far behind those of the south. The Turkish Cypriots lacked both the expertise and the manpower needed to develop the substantial assets left behind by the Greek Cypriots. The use of the Turkish lira has brought with it the economic ills that affect mainland Turkey—very high inflation and a shortage of investment funds. Products which in a united island are available locally have to be imported at much greater cost. As the north is not recognized, all international flights have to be routed via Turkey; no international airlines or tourist agencies, and no foreign banks except the Islamic Development Bank, operate in the north.

With regard to a possible settlement based on the reunification of the island, as the UN Secretary-General put it, the window of opportunity is closing.[10] With every year that passes the gap between the communities widens. Today the barriers that separate them are not only physical and economic but psychological and linguistic. A whole generation is growing up which has never met a member of the opposite community. Over the past eleven years parliamentary institutions and political parties, ranging from extreme right to Communist, have taken root in the north, adding new constraints to the search for a settlement.

In 1983 the Secretary-General, Perez de Cuellar, became personally involved in the negotiations. He himself had served in Cyprus for two years as the UN special representative. But the political climate was unfavorable to early progress. Western interests had received a new setback with the rise in Greece of Andreas Papandreou's socialist party, PASOK. Papandreou's philosophy that the real enemy of Greece is not the Soviet Union but Turkey is well known; on coming to power in October 1981 he committed himself to a crusade to mobilize international opinion against Turkey. The Cyprus issue again became top priority in Greek foreign policy and a stick with which to beat the Turks at every opportunity. After Papandreou's historic visit to Cyprus in 1982, the internationalization campaign rapidly gathered momentum.

Quiet diplomacy in Cyprus had been hampered by acrimonious debate in New York and elsewhere. For two years the Cyprus government was dissuaded from appealing to the UN General Assembly, but in May 1983 it launched a new appeal.

Over the years the Cyprus resolutions in the General Assembly have become increasingly unrealistic and often contradictory. The text under discussion at the Thirty-seventh General Assembly in 1983 was no exception. The British delegate urged restraint; the Canadian delegate called upon the nations contributing troops to the peace force to vote impartially. Both pleas went unheeded, and the motion was adopted by 105 votes to 4, with 25 abstentions.[11] More than two-thirds of the nations supporting the resolution were either from the Communist bloc or the nonaligned movement. No such consensus was to be found among the western powers. Among the European Economic Community members France voted with Greece; Portugal and Spain, candidates for membership of the EEC, did likewise. Some cohesion and unity of purpose might have been

Cyprus: A Failure in Western Diplomacy

expected from the nations which provided troops for the peace force. However, Australia, Austria, Finland, and Sweden voted for the motion, thereby compromising the peace force in Cyprus by undermining its reputation for evenhandedness.

The effect of the General Assembly debates has been to encourage false hopes among the Greek Cypriots and to cause a hardening of the Turkish attitude. But this time the debate set in motion the chain of events which led up to the Turkish declaration of an independent state. The damage done by the debate was consolidated a few weeks later by the visit to Cyprus of the president of the General Assembly, Hollai. Hollai, who had formerly been the Hungarian ambassador to Greece and Cyprus, refused to visit the Turkish Cypriot side.

The dust had to settle before the Secretary-General could make a new move, and his plan was not submitted to the Cypriot leaders until the autumn. But by that time the Turkish Cypriots had taken steps towards independence; and on 15 November they proclaimed the Turkish Republic of Northern Cyprus. The proclamation was conciliatory in tone and offered peace and friendship to the Greek Cypriots. Taken at face value, it left the door open to the eventual formation of a federal state with the Greek Cypriot sector.

All the parties to the Zurich agreements have been in breach of their provisions at some time or other. As the permanent British representative to the United Nations recently admitted, not one of them can claim the monopoly of virtue.[12] Yet in the eyes of the world it seems that, as George Orwell might have said, some are more illegal than others. The western powers joined the Soviet Union and the nonaligned movement in condemning the Turkish Cypriot action. Thirteen of the fifteen members of the Security Council adopted a resolution[13] which demanded the immediate withdrawal of the independence declaration and called upon all members not to recognize any Cyprus state other than the Republic of Cyprus. Pakistan voted against the resolution; Jordan abstained. To date, Turkey is the only country which has recognized the Turkish Republic of Northern Cyprus.

The western powers must, however, bear some responsibility for the Unilateral Declaration of Independence (UDI) which they have so vigorously condemned. Had they treated the Greek and Turkish Cypriot administrations from 1964 onwards as integral components of one government pending a new settlement, the Turkish Cypriots would have had much less reason to proclaim a separate state. But the policy of treating the Greek Cypriot administration as the legal government of the whole island forced the Turkish Cypriots into economic and political isolation and almost total dependence on Turkey. The consequent decline of western influence is a disturbing feature of present conditions in the north.

After eleven years of self-government the Turkish Cypriots saw independence as the only alternative to total assimilation by Turkey and, mistakenly, as a way out of their economic difficulties. But without either recognition or a settlement based on the reunification of the island, the economic outlook for the Turkish Cypriots is bleak.

The Turkish Cypriots have repeatedly said that the new status of the north is not a barrier to an eventual federal system. And after considerable delay Perez de Cuellar was able to resume his initiative. His efforts, combined with the pressure exerted by President Ronald Reagan on the Turkish government, resulted in a major breakthrough in December 1984. The Turkish Cypriots offered to reduce the territory under their control to twenty-nine percent of the island. In exchange, the Greek Cypriots made concessions over the constitutional structure. During the summit meeting held in New York the following January, Denktash agreed unconditionally to the Perez de Cuellar plan, but Kyprianou had reservations, which led to the collapse of the summit. For the first time in many years the Greek Cypriots got a bad press.

Kyprianou's handling of the intercommunal negotiations has long been the subject of controversy. The two strongest parties, the prowestern Democratic Rally and the Communist AKEL, favor a more realistic approach and have a common objective in their determination to remove him from office.

In the parliamentary elections of 8 December 1985 the Democratic Rally and AKEL failed to obtain the two-thirds of the seats which their leaders believed would have enabled them to amend the constitution and force the holding of presidential elections. Contrary to expectations, Kyprianou's Democratic Centre increased its strength and, with the support of Lyssarides's EDEK, again formed a minority government. At the end of 1985 a settlement of the Cyprus problem seemed as remote as ever.

But even if Perez de Cuellar could revive the December 1984 agreement on territory and constitution in a format acceptable to both communities, formidable difficulties still lie ahead. The final sticking points are likely to be Turkey's future role as a guarantor and the continuing presence in the north of a sizable Turkish garrison. The Turks are adamant that they can make no concessions over security. The Greek Cypriots, on the other hand, insist that there can be no security for them, and no settlement, until the Turkish troops are withdrawn.

It is often suggested that the West could play a more active role in resolving the dispute. But today, as in the past, Greek Cypriot expectations of the West are sharply at variance with those of the Turkish Cypriots. Given the complexities of the Cyprus conflict, it is perhaps not surprising that western policy should have failed. Indeed the verdict of history may well be that this was a situation in which no one could be expected to succeed.

NOTES

1. Assembly of Western European Union, 31st Ordinary Session, *Part I, May 1985, Minutes Official Report of Debates* (Paris); see M. Pierre Lagorce, 103.
2. Lt. Gen. Karayannis (Retd.), *The Cyprus Question,* "Ethnikos Kyrix," 6 June 1965 (Athens).
3. Security Council resolution 186 (4 March 1964).
4. Ibrahim Salih, *Cyprus: The Impact of Diverse Nationalism on a State* (University of Alabama Press, 1978), 144–52.

5. Security Council resolution 193 (9 August 1964).
6. *Cyprus Mail*, 1 January 1968.
7. *Report of the Select Committee on Cyprus*, HMSO, 8 April 1976, p. 13.
8. *Cyprus Intercommunal Talks* (Nicosia: Public Information Office, July 1981), 27.
9. Necati Ertekun, *The Cyprus Dispute* (Lefkosa: Rustem & Bro., 1984) 321–34.
10. UN document S/15502, p. 13.
11. Security Council resolution 253 (13 May 1983).
12. See Sir John Thomson, UN documents S/PV 2538, pp. 24–25; S/PV 2539, 16–17.
13. Security Council resolution 541 (18 November 1983).

Education—
The International Dimension
John Brademas

It was in 1959 that I became the first native-born American of Greek origin to take a seat in the Congress of the United States. During twenty-two years of service on Capitol Hill, I took part in writing most of the legislation now on the statute books to support education at all levels as well as the arts and humanities, libraries, and museums.

Since July of 1981, I have been president of New York University, the largest private university in the nation, with 47,000 students in fourteen schools and divisions, an annual budget of more than $800 million, and located in the commercial, cultural, and communications capital of the world, New York City. Because what happens in New York City has such a powerful impact not only on our own country but on the entire world, and, because of the importance of the subject, I will direct my comments to the theme of international education—learning about the rest of the world.

It must be obvious to us all that none of the challenges of our time is more urgent, or more difficult, than building a structure of relationships among the nations of the world that will prevent war and encourage peace. Surely one of the ways, although not the only way, to achieve this objective is through the use of human reason, and that means education.

The globe on which we live is, in the scheme of things, small and its inhabitants are interdependent. Terrorism in the Middle East, conflict in Central America, the threat of civil war in the Philippines, tensions on Cyprus and in the Eastern Mediterranean are all developments that reach far across international borders. How well are we preparing Americans to understand other nations, other cultures, other peoples? In my view, we are not doing very well. There is simply no question that the people of the United States, in whose hands for better or for worse, lies much of the responsibility for building a peaceful and stable world, must do a far better job of learning about those who populate other parts of this planet.

Eight years ago, a twenty-five-member Commission on Foreign Language and International Studies, chaired by James A. Perkins, former president of Cornell University, reported to President Jimmy Carter on America's "scandalous incompetence" in foreign languages. The commission members declared themselves "profoundly alarmed" by the results of their inquiry. Here are just three of their findings:

1. More than forty percent of twelfth graders were unable to place Egypt correctly on a map, while more than twenty percent were equally ignorant of the locations of France or China.
2. Only fifteen percent of American high school students studied a foreign language, down from twenty-four percent in 1965.
3. Over 10,000 English-speaking Japanese business representatives were on assignment in the United States, but there were fewer than 900 American counterparts in Japan; of those, only a handful had a working knowledge of Japanese.

As we all know, during the last few years there has been a veritable wave of reports on the performance of American schools, colleges, and universities. Most of these studies deplore our deficiencies in teaching modern foreign languages and educating students about other countries and cultures.

In 1983, I was chairman of the Subcommittee on Graduate Education of the National Commission on Student Financial Assistance. This twelve member bipartisan commission was created by Congress to review student aid programs and offer suggestions for improving them.

Education—The International Dimension

Our commission was disheartened to learn that between 1969 and 1978, federal expenditures for university-based foreign affairs research declined from $20.3 million annually to $8.5 million. The commission also took note of a study by the National Council on Foreign Language and International Studies, which documented a serious lack in this country of experts on the cultures, economies, and foreign policies of Asia, sub-Saharan Africa, the Middle East, the Soviet Union, and Eastern Europe. In preparing our report on graduate education, the commission members spoke to two former directors of the Central Intelligence Agency. Both William Colby and Stansfield Turner blamed Americans' lack of expert knowledge about Vietnam and Iran for serious intelligence shortcomings in those countries, and both men said that our ignorance of Latin America appeared "almost boundless." Not surprisingly, our commission unanimously recommended that federal funds for research, instruction, and graduate work in a wide range of languages and cultures be significantly increased, and that federal support for American scholars to study abroad also be expanded.

In November of 1984, William J. Bennett, then chairman of the National Endowment for the Humanities and later Secretary of Education, issued a report critical of the state of the humanities on American campuses. This document cited a sharp decline since 1966 in college entrance and graduation requirements in foreign languages. In February of 1985, the Association of American Colleges published its analysis of the baccalaureate degree. The AAC Committee called our "foreign language incompetence" a "national embarrassment" and included "international and multicultural experience" as one area in its minimum required program of study.

Beyond these studies and surveys, two other recent reports have focused exclusively on international education. The first, *Critical Needs in International Education: Recommendations for Action*, was produced by the National Advisory Board on International Education Programs, a panel of scholars, government and business leaders, and others. The report declares, "Our nation's indifference to foreign languages and cultures is unique among the advanced industrial countries and our performance in these areas lags behind that of many developing countries." The second study, *Beyond Growth: The Next State in Language and Area Studies,* was prepared by the Association of American Universities for the U.S. Department of Defense. The research team, headed by Richard Lambert of the University of Pennsylvania, explained that, "Secretary of Defense Caspar Weinberger chose language and area studies along with mathematics and science as one of the domains of higher education he felt was in greatest jeopardy of decline and of greatest interest to the nation and the Department of Defense."

The AAU study finds "vital gaps" in both research and teaching in foreign language and area studies. Financial aid programs are not producing an adequate supply of persons knowledgeable about other countries; students need to be trained better and longer. Of interest to friends of Greece is a summary, appended to the AAU report and prepared by William B. Bader of SRI International, of the nation's needs in western European studies. Bader observes that, "Far fewer Americans today endeavor to understand the intricacies of European affairs than twenty years ago," and goes on to point out the neglect of the countries of southern Europe in favor of the study of the United Kingdom, France, and Germany. Bader says that the American academic community has too few people who qualify as expert on contemporary Greece with, he charges, none in the United States government.

Whatever the reasons for the troubled state of international studies in this country, at one time it seemed clear that the nation was willing to take steps to overcome our ignorance. The Soviet launching of Sputnik in 1957 shocked us into a reevaluation of the quality of American education. Our response was the National Defense Education Act, an effort, advocated by President Dwight D. Eisenhower and supported by a Democratic Congress, to regain our international leadership in science and technology. Through Title VI of NDEA, we also sought to enhance our capacities in foreign languages and area studies.

However, we have consistently failed to provide adequate funds for these programs. For example, the International Education Act of 1966, of which I was author in Congress and which authorized grants to colleges and universities in the United States to support study and research about foreign countries, cultures, and important issues in international affairs, was also ignored in the appropriations process. Although President Lyndon B. Johnson signed this act into law nearly two decades ago, Congress failed to vote funds to turn our sound intentions into effective action. Had these commitments to international studies been implemented, the United States might have been far better prepared to deal with problems our country has suffered in Iran, Vietnam, Central America, and elsewhere.

I must note that America's colleges and universities are themselves not without blame. In the 1960s many of them responded to student demands for greater flexibility and "relevance" in their studies by eliminating foreign language requirements.

Today it is distressing to see how the present administration in Washington has embarked on a drive to slash funds for schools, colleges, universities, and other institutions of education and culture, including monies for programs crucial to international studies and research. For example, the Reagan administration has repeatedly attempted to eliminate federal support for Title VI, which is now part of the Higher Education Act. So even as many of us have been working to defeat the administration's attempts, equally wrongheaded and dangerous, to reduce or eliminate financial aid for hundreds of thousands of college and university students, we have also had to struggle against efforts to weaken our capacity to prepare more people to be knowledgeable about other areas of the world.

I do not want to sound wholly alarmist or negative; I see several signs of hope. In 1981 Republicans and Democrats in Congress joined in a successful fight to prevent drastic cuts in the Fulbright academic exchanges and several companion programs. This crisis proved dramatically that there is a strong and vocal constituency in America in support of such efforts. And in each of three years, Congress has fended off Reagan's determination to kill funds for Title VI international education programs. Indeed, in recent years, federally financed education exchanges have undergone a dramatic shift in fortune. In 1985, the administration requested $159 million for the Fulbright and other exchange programs administered by the United States Information Agency, an increase of twenty-two percent over current levels.

Beyond these developments, I have been heartened by some other initiatives. Many universities—including Harvard, the University of Pennsylvania, Emory, Middlebury College, and the University of Massachusetts—are reinstituting required courses in languages and other international studies. A recent Modern Language Association study indicated that, in a reversal of a twelve year trend, enrollments in foreign language courses at American colleges and universities are now on the upswing.

I am pleased to say that both NYU and Ball State University are in the vanguard of this return to rigor. Not only must all NYU undergraduate art and science students achieve competency in a foreign language, but since 1981, our students must take at least an introductory course in a non-Western culture. One of the achievements of President John Worthen's first year at Ball State was to create a Center for International Programs. The new center will attract more foreign students, strengthen international offerings, and expand foreign exchange programs.

As an American of Greek ancestry, I have been particularly interested in the development of Greek studies on American campuses. Studies should include the classical Greek heritage and its transmission from ancient Greece to modern times. Although the great creative period of ancient Greece spanned but four centuries, the eighth through the fifth centuries B.C., Greek thought and civilization have shaped our world for millennia. One need only read *The Legacy of Greece,* edited by the classicist M. I. Finley of Cambridge University, to understand how pervasive and persistent the influence of Greece in western civilization has been. Says one contributor, R. R. Bolger, "When one considers our indebtedness to ancient Greece, one is struck by the variety of the elements that were borrowed." Bolger cites, for example, the Pythagorean theorem, the dramatic unities, the three orders of architecture, and the legend of Oedipus. Think, he says, of the several names and enduring works: the epics of Homer, the poetry of Sappho, the history of Herodotus and Thucydides, the philosophy and politics of Plato and Aristotle.

Bolger goes on to show that in literature, art, and philosophy, virtually all later ages followed Greek models. The Romans, of course, borrowed substantially but even the Dark and Middle Ages learned from Greece. Bolger finds Greek strands in Augustine's *City of God,* in the early Christian hymn writers, and in the Carolingian poets. Avicenna, the greatest of medieval Arab thinkers, looked to Aristotle, and from Greek sources flowed the famous tales of the *Thousand and One Nights.*

Yet it was not until the Renaissance that the Romans' passion for Greece was rekindled throughout Europe. With the thirteenth century came a flowering of philhellenism. The first person to recognize the genius of Homer and Plato was Petrarch. Ronsard read Pindar; Racine, Euripides; and John Milton studied a number of Greek writers. Lucian influenced Erasmus, Rabelais, Ben Jonson, and Cervantes; Plutarch inspired Montaigne and Shakespeare.

The classics became in the eighteenth century a cornerstone of higher education in England. Cambridge awarded prizes for proficiency in classical studies. As Bolger says, "Ability to reproduce a passage from Burke in the style of Demosthenes, to make Hume write as Thucydides had written, emerged as the hallmark of scholarly achievement." Tests of such capacities were adopted for examination at Oxford after 1800 and at Cambridge after 1824. The nineteenth-century champion of classical education was, of course, Matthew Arnold.

As love of Greece shaped other cultures for two thousand years, philhellenism was a central force in the young American republic. Certainly the great American universities, like their European counterparts, revered the classics. Classical Greek studies flourished at my alma mater, Harvard, since its founding in 1636, and at Princeton since its establishment in the following century. And, to qualify for admission to its "full classical and scientific course," in 1832, one year after the founding of New York University, students there were required by the Governing Council to "be acquainted with a Greek grammar" and to "have read . . . the Greek New Testament, the books of Xenophon and two books of the Iliad."

Beyond the impact of Greece on American intellectual life, our Founding Fathers looked to ancient Greece for guidance in devising our system of government. In an address at the Center for Hellenic Studies in Washington, the distinguished American writer Archibald MacLeish noted:

> What is philosophically true of "all men" in Jefferson's preamble [to the Declaration of Independence] had been historically true of every man — or at least of every citizen — in Pericles' Athens. The citizens of Athens were not subjects of the state: they were men inviolable in their quality as men. And so, in Jefferson's Declaration, should the Americans be.

When the promise of America swept across the ocean, it provided an example for many other peoples, including the Greeks themselves. In 1821, my ancestors declared their independence from the Ottoman Empire. The subsequent War of Independence captured the American imagination, fueled a resurgence of philhellenism, and changed the course of Greek studies in this country. Statesmen, scholars, and writers were fired by the Greek cause. Speeches were made before Congress by President James Monroe and Senators Daniel Webster and Henry Clay. Like Byron and Shelley in Europe, dozens of American poets such as William Cullen Bryant elegized the Greeks. Several Americans actually fought alongside the Greek insurgents. Among them was Samuel Gridley Howe, a professor at Harvard. In his book, *An Historical Sketch of the Greek Revolution,* published in 1828, Howe expressed the sentiment of many American intellectuals: "The Greek Revolution was one of the most important, and certainly the most interesting political event of our age."

It is not surprising that at this time we saw the beginning

of modern, in addition to classical, Greek studies at colleges and universities in the United States. At Harvard scholars, students, and public officials, inspired by the Greek War of Independence, produced a burst of philhellenic writing. These materials were a significant factor in the development of the Modern Greek Collection of the Harvard University Library, which today is a resource for neohellenic studies unequalled outside Greece. Then as now, Americans of Greek descent, as well as those who were not, supported Greek studies. Among the early benefactors of the Harvard Greek collection were the Greek-American scholar Evangelinos Apostolides Sophocles and American philhellenes Cornelius Felton and Edward Everett.

Even as Harvard was building its Greek library collection, it began in the 1820s to offer courses in the modern Greek language. Later in the nineteenth century, under the aegis of Evangelinos Sophocles, Harvard became a world center for the study of modern Greek. Professor Sophocles wrote the first modern Greek grammar and first modern Greek lexicon, yet his attempts to establish a permanent program in neohellenic studies failed. The truth is that although courses on classical Greece have thrived in the United States, modern Greek studies have not taken hold until recent years.

Several factors have stimulated a new interest in contemporary Greece. First, the works of modern Greek writers such as Nikos Kazantzakis, Constantine Cavafy, and the Nobel Laureates in poetry, George Seferis and Odysseus Elytis, became available in English. Second, in what has been called the "roots" syndrome, Greek-Americans, like other ethnic groups, began to feel a new pride in their identity. And finally, more and more Americans have been traveling to Greece.

In a climate more conducive to neohellenic studies, American colleges and universities have begun to offer courses and lectures on contemporary Greece. And, as Charles C. Moskos explains in his book, *Greek Americans,* "The driving force behind such efforts has been due to Greek-born scholars who have settled in this country, second-generation Greek-American professors and modern Greek literary critics of non-Greek origin."

The first formal attempt to bring modern Greek studies to American campuses was the Center for Neo-Hellenic Studies founded in 1965 at the University of Texas by Professor George Arnakis. The center, like many later efforts a one-man enterprise, did not survive after the death of Arnakis. Hopes for building a sustained interest in contemporary Greek society and culture advanced significantly with the formation in 1968 of the Modern Greek Studies Association, an organization of approximately 600 scholars, students, and philhellenes devoted to the encouragement of the study of modern Greece both here and abroad. The principal activities of the MGSA include the publication of a biannual *Journal of Modern Greek Studies* and the sponsorship of symposia every two years which deal with such themes as the Greek War of Independence, forces shaping modern Greece, and contemporary Greek literature.

Two of the five presidents of MGSA have been Americans who are not of Greek origin. The first MGSA president, my close friend Edmund Keeley of Princeton University, has done as much as anyone in this country to make Americans aware of modern Greek literature. A former Fulbright scholar in Greece, whose brother Robert was named U.S. ambassador to Greece, Keeley has produced definitive translations of Cavafy, Seferis, Elytis, and several other modern Greek writers. Another former non-Greek president of MGSA is Peter Bien, a professor of English at Dartmouth.

Both these ardent philhellenes have poignantly described the struggle to develop modern Greek studies as an academic discipline. Keeley wrote in 1976: "Working in modern Greek literature is a lonely enterprise; few know its riches, very few teach the subject, even fewer come to the literature as scholars or critics, especially in the United States." Bien said in 1978: "For seventeen years I have been *sneaking* modern Greek works into my courses by hook or by crook in no less than three departments . . . we who profess neglected literatures are beggars in our universities."

Fortunately the situation for neohellenic studies has brightened in recent years, with several encouraging signs of progress. First, the George Seferis Chair of Modern Greek Studies was created at Harvard in 1975, the first such endowed professorship in the United States. The establishment of such chairs elevates the prestige of a discipline, helps attract and retain first-class scholars, and ensures the continuation of courses in a particular field. Boston University, Queens College, Rutgers University, and Indiana University all hope to create chairs in Greek studies as well.

Second, there has been a sharp upsurge in enrollments in Greek language courses at American colleges and universities, from nearly 700 students, both undergraduate and graduate, in 1977 to almost 1,000 students in 1983, an increase of more than forty percent. Finally, there are more programs and courses in neohellenic studies on American campuses, including efforts at Ball State, Barnard College, Dartmouth, Harvard, Kent State, Ohio State, Princeton, Queens College, Regis College, San Francisco State, the University of Florida, and the University of Minnesota.

It is not surprising that the largest such program is at Queens College in New York City. There are 300,000 Greek-Americans in New York, nearly 100,000 of whom live in Astoria in the borough of Queens. The 2,000 Greek-American students at Queens College provide a natural constituency for its Byzantine and modern Greek studies program. Although many of the nearly 600 students who annually enroll in these courses at Queens College are of Greek descent, many are not.

It is more surprising—and splendid—that Ball State University and, with but *two* Greek-American families, the town of Muncie, have been so responsive to Greek studies. The Hellenic studies program and these Brademas Lectures have, I am pleased to say, attracted the world's preeminent scholars of classical and contemporary Greece. I do not have to look far to find the people who have made these activities so successful. One of course is John Koumoulides, but I must also applaud the generous philhellenes who comprise the Friends of Greek Studies at Ball State. Certainly, the programs here and at other colleges and universities in this country are helping in important ways to prepare Americans for work and life in a world that will never be narrow again.

Each of us must enter the battle that continues to be waged in Washington, D.C., over support of our schools, colleges, and universities, including international studies and research. None of us can afford the luxury of disdain for political discourse. We need to remind President Reagan that when he attacks education, he is really threatening both our prospects for a growing and more competitive economy and the security of the United States in a dangerous world. This president, who has placed economic prosperity and a strong national defense at the top of his agenda, apparently fails to see the close connection between the achievement of these goals and the health of the schools, colleges, and universities of the United States.

It must be evident that so perilous is our common life on this precious earth that we must, all of us, commit every fiber of our minds and spirits to the quest for a stable peace and a world of freedom and justice. To be able effectively to pursue this most important of objectives, however, we must know and understand one another, at least know and understand more than we do today. The distinguished American statesman who gave his name to the Fulbright program put the case I am making in eloquent words. Said Senator J. William Fulbright: "Education is a slow-moving but powerful force. It may not be fast enough or strong enough to save us from catastrophe, but it is the strongest force available."